FINDING NATURE

IN PHILADELPHIA

# *Vanished Gardens*

SHARON WHITE

The University of Georgia Press
Athens and London

Published by the University of Georgia Press
Athens, Georgia 30602
www.ugapress.org
© 2008 by Sharon White
All rights reserved
Designed by Mindy Basinger Hill
Set in 11.25/15 Adobe Jenson Pro
Printed and bound by Thomson-Shore
The paper in this book meets the guidelines for
permanence and durability of the Committee on
Production Guidelines for Book Longevity of the
Council on Library Resources.

Printed in the United States of America
12 11 10 09 08 C 5 4 3 2 1

Library of Congress Cataloging-in-Publication Data
White, Sharon, 1953–
  Vanished gardens : finding nature in Philadelphia /
Sharon White.
        p.      cm.
  Includes bibliographical references.
  ISBN-13: 978-0-8203-3156-0 (hardcover : alk. paper)
  ISBN-10: 0-8203-3156-2 (hardcover : alk. paper)
  1. Historic gardens—Pennsylvania—Philadelphia.
  2. Plants—Pennsylvania—Philadelphia. I. Title.
  SB451.34.P4W45 2008
  712.09748'11—dc22   2008014141

British Library Cataloging-in-Publication Data available

Title page and part title page image © Hélène Vallée / istockphoto.com

IN MEMORY OF ALMITRA DAVID

*"I leave to the various futures*

*(not to all) my garden of forking paths."*

JORGE LUIS BORGES

# Contents

# Springettsbury

## THE PRETTIEST
## OLD-FASHIONED GARDEN

# 1. Grapefruit

MY FIRST GARDEN WAS TROPICAL. I planted it in my great aunt's backyard in Florida with dust and rocks and dry thick leaves as big as my hand. Light filtered through grapefruit trees. Banana trees rustled in the warm wind. I played there for hours alone with my dolls. One morning I made a water garden in a small dusty pool bordered with stones. I pretended there were seahorses swimming in the pool. As I played I could smell the sweet sharp fragrance of grapefruit ripe in their rough bright skins. My aunt thought I was unhappy. I was such a quiet little girl content to play near the yellow light of the citrus trees.

Now I live near a wide shallow river on the very edge of the coastal plain that extends north to Philadelphia. I know the sweep of shiny marsh and sandy beach that flows up out of the soft air of Florida to the waters of the river near my house. The sea washes in there, too.

I garden here in a city rich in gardens and rich in the history of gardens. My house sits not far from a place where Thomas Penn grew lime trees in wooden tubs wintered in a greenhouse and summered outside in a pattern of five. When he was in England, his gardener sent him the fruit from his citrus trees. I grow a miniature orange tree with soft little fruit, good for marmalade, in my bedroom in the winter, and when the weather warms I move it outside to the deck.

Sometimes my gardens here are like the first one I concocted when I was nine, more dust and sticks and large leathery leaves than anything else. Some early summers, though, the lilies I grow are as large as grapefruit and as sweet.

All up and down the Schuylkill River near our house are gardens that the wind and rain and years of weather have swept clean.

Swatches of land where men or women gardened and then died or moved away leaving their gardens to the elements. We live surrounded by the pieces of gardens long gone to weed or water or pavement. Each day I walk over their bones on my route through the gardens that slope down to the road above the river. I pass ornate fountains hidden under branches, a rectangle of formal garden bordered by boxwood in a thicket behind a large square house that a pirate built for his retirement, brownstone stairs that lead nowhere, a yucca along the edge of the road—the last part of an elaborate pleasure garden—the old battered trunks of huge trees split off at the top, sprouting suckers, roads that wind along the river to gardens sold to graveyards, mausoleums built over soil where the owners once planted rare trees imported from exotic places.

I suppose everyone has ghost gardens in their history even if they don't think about them all that much. The memory of these cultivated places disturbs me in odd seasons. The tight miniature bud of a snowdrop, a sweep of lawn down to a wild bit of brush, the bare backyard of my grandmother's apartment, weeds grown up in the corners near the garage, my mother's long garden on Jillson Circle when I was seven, full of iris—the smell of longing as I walk past the iris in the community garden, fresh, thick, curled purple—and blackeyed susans and small red roses, the sugary taste of a scallion from my uncle's garden, just after he had peeled the dirt off and dipped it into a handful of sugar for me, my other grandmother's opium poppies and cinnamon smelling pinks, the only flowers she grew in her clipped backyard.

The more I live in my corner of Philadelphia, the more it seems that the city is an extensive garden, a bit wild in parts. Who gardened here before me in the fertile soil along the river and on the rocky hills of the Piedmont?

## 2. Boxwood

ONCE THERE WAS A GARDEN HERE where I write, an intricate labyrinth bordered in clipped boxwood, the Labyrinthine Garden. Our house sits on the edge of the vanished labyrinth, part of a pleasure garden open for only a few years in the early nineteenth century. From sometime in the 1820s to 1833 there was a pavilion and a narrow pagoda called the Temple of Confucius, 110 feet high. The pagoda was a tower with a succession of curved spring-green roofs, bells on the tip of each tier. A grassy lawn circled the base of the pagoda. The labyrinth was sunk below the lawn and wound around the pagoda. Visitors walked through the labyrinth to the pagoda at the center. Roses or peonies bloomed against fences of diagonal latticework. In front of the pagoda was a building designed in the Chinese style with its own curved roof and lattice at the windows and a red stable to the east for carriages and horses.

In the late summer heat people came out from town to enjoy the cool garden on a hill above the city. From the tower they had a fine view. The streets then went right up to the river, sloping down from the garden.

In the engraving I looked at yesterday fashionably dressed ladies wore Empire-waist dresses and bonnets like halos around their faces. A child dressed like his father and uncle in a tall hat and a coat with long black tails stood near them. Inside they could expect strawberries and ice cream, amusements and drinks, and a collection of tall leafy trees. Along the road that was Coates Street, now Fairmount, a solitary elm arched away from the garden in the picture. A mansion gone now for two hundred years, the Samson Mansion, stood across from the garden, and down the street on Francis Lane a farm advertised strawberries and ice cream. All the movement was toward the river and the waterworks on a hill west of the garden. All the artifice is inside, hidden behind the first building, green and red and white. You can see the tips of the leafy trees, perhaps a few fir trees or cypresses, and arched canopies of maple, elm, tulip, or sycamore. Along the road the grass is rough, and the lithographer has engraved a few large soft leaves near the elm, mullein perhaps. A boy is running with his arm outstretched, hand held palm up, away from the garden toward the river. Someone is snapping a whip above the ears of his spirited horses. A man is galloping on a slim horse, a carriage is pulling up to the gate.

# 3. Daffodil

I'M PLANTING DAFFODILS AT DUSK at the edge of the Labyrinthine Garden. Around me people move through the chilled air at
five, one leaf or two brushes their shoulders as the yellow leaves float
to the pavement. The pruning of light and leaf and heat and flower,
of nail, of teeth, of hair, that old repetition of the season closing itself
down, begins again. One month and then winter will set itself up to
freeze the river, perhaps, and coat the trees' limbs with ice and fill the
deck with snow if we're lucky. But each bulb is a cliché as I plant, that
fat nugget of yellow light or white and salmon or lemon and cream.

As I pull the dirt aside and stuff each bulb into a pocket of soil I see
other daffodils and spring bulbs long withered or eaten or dug up. A
filbert orchard in Oregon where I once lived by the wild McKenzie
River where the daffodils bloomed in bright clumps all March in the
constant drizzle of the northwest, or the yellow aconites in England
in the park near my flat, the snowdrops lifting their heavy white and
green heads to the silvery Oxford light. I planted snowdrops here
too, a row in the back patio wedged between the bulbs of *Narcissus
poeticus* and lilies.

I'm planting the bulbs in a new raised bed constructed around
one of the elms that border our house and bend over the sidewalk.
My husband, Scott, and our neighbor, George, put it together this
afternoon and we've just filled it with a second bag of compressed
bedding soil. I'm putting the bulbs to bed. Patting each crinkly tuber
down. Tomorrow I'll water them in.

The daffodil is a conqueror's bulb. They weren't growing here when
the first settlers sailed up the river. Or perhaps they were, for Claire
Haughton in her book *Green Immigrants* tells me that when women

came over from England in 1619 as wives for the soldiers at Jamestown, they brought daffodil bulbs tucked in their apron pockets with seeds and roots wrapped in moss. Daffodils grew in many other early gardens north and south, and the settlers called them old names like daffydowndilly, hooped skirts, codlins-in-cream, Lenten lilies, and butter-and-eggs.

When his Quaker friend Peter Collinson sent John Bartram, the King's Botanist and good friend of Benjamin Franklin, double white daffodils from England, Bartram told him they were common in Pennsylvania. The daffodils grew wild in the fields around his garden on the lower Schuylkill River at Kingsessing.

Galen, physician to the Roman legions in the northern frontier during the time of Marcus Aurelius, wrote that the "slimy" juice of the narcissus "would glue together great wounds, cuts, and gashes." He ordered that every soldier should carry bulbs with him as medicine, planting the wild Mediterranean bulbs this way in the north.

I'm hoping that the little squirrel who digs in the pots in the backyard and the edges of the tree boxes will ignore the daffodils. She won't eat them, I know, but she might mess them up. If I ate them I'd be in trouble. Daffodil sap can irritate your hands. Now, the daffodil is classified as poisonous. Animals stay away from them. Even deer won't dig them up. If I ate a daffodil shoot and the sweet white bulb, I might experience "difficulty in swallowing, as well as nausea, vomiting, diarrhea, sweating, trembling and even convulsions." I might die. I'd have problems with other plants in the garden we've assembled here if I ate them: the English ivy (I've been pulling it up since we moved in) or the holly berries or the foxglove.

Our brick row house, built around 1900, was a candy shop until about twenty years ago. Once a woman sold cigars here. It's three stories and narrow. The front window is wide and juts out over the sidewalk. We wonder if the old glass might break and shatter. A long window runs the height of the house on the side, many-paned and brittle too. Our door opens from the dining room to the street. If you stood on the sidewalk you could see straight through to the back patio. When I sit at the kitchen counter I can see air through the mail slot. On cold mornings Scott stuffs a rag sock in the opening.

Blessed in odd ways, we live on a corner that attracts trash but catches morning light. Our third floor brushes the branches of the elm like a tree house.

We moved here not long ago after many years living in a small town in Massachusetts. Here the tight blooms of roses glow in their wound paper funnels piled on tables on the sidewalk. Asparagus, slim and green in its box, sits in front of the shuttered stores in the morning.

I cultivate several gardens. Pots on the deck off our bedroom are filled with lavender and rhubarb and roses and herbs. I've experimented with tomatoes and baby popcorn and eggplant. Tiny black rats nibbled the tomatoes last summer so I've given up on raising vegetables on the deck. Along the side of the house I squeezed a long garden into a planter filled with ivy when we first moved in. Now we have pink lilies and striped daylilies and a clump of white iris that hasn't bloomed yet and meadow rue and coreopsis and a green columbine I love with delicate yellow stamens. On summer mornings I crush a leaf of cascading lemon thyme or soft lavender and admire a dark purple clematis that grows on a trellis against a long window.

In the little patio off the living room we grow bamboo in pots and exotic elephant ears and pink and yellow foxgloves in a bed along the fence we share with our neighbor. There are two small holly trees that the robins peck clean of their shiny red berries in the winter, and a little pink rose in an elaborate terra cotta pot, like an amphora, fat in the middle and set on a pedestal.

A few blocks from here we have a tiny plot in the community garden where we experiment with pumpkins and gourds and Indian corn and fancy chard. Right now the garden is filled with zinnias and cosmos, the small orange kind, and the large, heavy heads of sunflowers.

Our neighborhood is north from the center of the city on a hill called Fair Mount on the old maps. When our house was constructed this wasn't a fashionable part of Philadelphia. Actors and toolmakers built brownstone or brick mansions decorated with stone lions and iron fences on farmland, and soon the brick sidewalks were replaced by shiny stone rectangles, a sign of the new prosperity.

We live on the edge of the grand-sounding Piedmont, the low rocky shelf that extends from the Appalachians and Blue Ridge in the west to the Atlantic coastal plain in the east and south from New York City to Montgomery, Alabama. Colonists settled at the mouth of the major rivers here then sailed up the placid rivers of the Atlantic plain as far as they could to establish trading outposts for goods from the interior. Here the rivers meet the jagged ledges of rocks that are the rivers' navigable limits. Boatmen called these abrupt falls or rapids the "fall line." Wealthy colonists settled along the alluvial lowlands where the soil was rich sandy loam, and less prosperous settlers went inland to the hills where the rolling landscape reminded them of the foothills of southern Europe, the Piedmont.

The soft silty landscape of the coastal plain ends at the fall line at the bottom of our street, where the Schuylkill River once cascaded over the rapids. And like the landscape our lives have come to the border of something new. Stone and sand, uplift and sediment.

Sometimes the river smells familiar—like a small lake in August, fish in the shallows, barely a boat in sight, a slight ripple on the shining surface. When I walk up the hill from the river I see crates of lemons and pomegranates at the corner store, their tight skins caged behind wooden bars.

We're surrounded by churches—St. Hedwig's, St. Nicholas, St. Ludwig's, and St. Francis Xavier. The corner west of us is anchored by a Catholic school. Next to the school stands St. Francis Xavier Church, and down the street a convent where members of the Holy Spirit Adoration Sisters cultivate their own walled garden at the end of the block and a tiny pair of gardens with giant lilies in the front yard of the Chapel of Divine Love. Sometimes I sit in the quiet chapel as the sisters kneel behind their gold screen and pray, their pink habits spread in a fan around their bent knees.

On Sundays I admire the stained glass windows in the sanctuary of St. Francis Xavier's, the devotion to Mary. I listen to the sermon. Father Georges reminds me that the physical world is slipping away. I'm not really smelling the sweet sharp taste of the orange I hold up to my nose.

This dusk is indistinct tonight, glowing not with sunset or coming mist, but with pure hazy light that hampers me as I try to figure out where to plant the next bulb. I've been feeling hazy all day. I woke early and went off for a walk with a friend who has lived here her whole life.

"Was there really a swimming pool under the water?" I asked her when we stopped on our walk up the west side of the Schuylkill and looked at the nineteenth-century waterworks still suspended in restoration.

"Well, maybe not, but I was little girl, and I looked down from those windows over there and maybe it was an aquarium and my father or mother said 'Oh look there's someone swimming.' Maybe it was just someone looking up from the rooms below. I don't know."

I've been confused today thinking my father was still alive but he's not. When we first moved here his death caught up to me. As I unpacked my shoes and belts and folded scarves I unpacked thoughts of him stored for a year. It has nothing to do with the season—he died in the summer—or the place—we never came here together. I don't really think of him any more or less in the fall. Maybe it's the sense of insubstantial air.

Some day all of this could disappear. Maybe it has already: the crumpled trash, smashed plastic bottles, potato chip bags, torn condoms, Pepsi cans, cigarette boxes, dirty clothes, ripped cups, cigarette ends, foil wrappers, broken branches, fallen leaves—bright yellow, buffed brown—on the bridge as we walk across the river that once flowed to a vast marsh and now winds through the city—the blazing bushes on the edge of the river, shining silver branches, the swimming pool that may not have existed at all, the little girl holding her father's hand as they looked at the river. Long ago, people lived here at the mouth of the river. The women farming, hoeing their corn and beans and squash with a clamshell hoe, the men hunting for elk and deer and small animals. In the spring they burned the underbrush to encourage browse and moved to the place where they fished or hunted migratory birds. The marsh then was fifty-seven hundred acres, and the people who lived there called their settlement Pachsegink, "In the Valley." They had vanished up the Schuylkill by the time William Penn arrived to negotiate his purchase of their land, part of a landscape they called Lenapehoking.

The edge of the glacier, the braided delta of Darby Creek, and the Schuylkill and Delaware Rivers shine in the low fall sun. The tall trees and meadows came later, cultivated and coaxed by the many people who lived here before the first Europeans came up the river and built their houses, and fenced their land, and planted their daffodils.

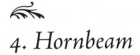

# 4. Hornbeam

WHEN I RUN ONCE OR TWICE around the baseball fields at
the end of our street I'm on the edge of one kind of landscape and
another, my feet poised at the very edge of the coastal plain as I run.
My walk home brings me up the hill, a line of rock that extends from
here south to Alabama. I'm on the intersecting line, too, of one history
and another. We live on the edge of William Penn's Springettsbury, a
large tract of land he reserved for his family at the original northern
border of the city. I'm running on the soil of Springettsbury.

Penn didn't live here, but his son Thomas built a house on the
sloping land in the late 1730s. His estate included a brick house with
a main wing and a kitchen and rooms for servants in the back, a
greenhouse, and a long walk down a small valley to a stream. Nearby
ran a path to a fish pond where visitors admired the glitter of goldfish
in the clear water. They could walk in an orchard and a deer park.

Visitors described a "wilderness of trees," a pruned woodland,
fashionable in Britain at this time, a maze of hornbeam trees, and
formal gardens. What would it be like to wander in a labyrinth of
hornbeam, winding through the corridors of pleached and cropped
branches with their lime green leaves in the early heat of a Philadelphia June?

Penn planted spruce hedges and clipped them into fanciful topiary,
out of fashion then in England. He bordered his gardens with fences
and decorated them with painted benches and gates. His striped
tulips bloomed near ranunculus, perhaps soft and the color of rasp-
berry like the flower I grow in a pot on the deck, each petal a flute of
saturated color spilled out on the cold spring air.

He built one of the first greenhouses in Philadelphia. In the large brick structure, he wintered his oranges, lemons, limes, and citrons. He tried to grow jasmine but the sweet-blooming plant didn't survive the cold winter.

In their essay on Springettsbury in the *Journal of the New England Garden History Society*, Elizabeth McLean and Mark Reinberger write that Thomas Penn was the proprietor of the colony after his father's death, but like his father he spent only a few years living in Pennsylvania. Business and family problems pulled him back to England and he never returned. Thomas, unlike his father, was fond of an extravagant lifestyle and more interested in designing an elaborate villa and pleasure garden at Springettsbury than Penn had been at his house and garden at Pennsbury Manor on the Delaware north of Philadelphia. I like to think of Thomas Penn as a rebellious son. He abandoned his father's Quaker past and became an Anglican, a religion more attuned to the pleasures of the body. His house, he noted, would be appropriate to his status as the "first man in the place he resides in."

Thomas Penn designed his house and gardens to reflect the fashion in England of a landscape with natural contours and views framed with trees or formal hedges. He thought of his land as an estate and not a working farm, unlike his father and other early colonists. His gardener was James Alexander, one of the first professional gardeners in America.

Peter Collinson sent him horse chestnuts, cornelian cherries, boxwood trees, "long-blowing honeysuckel," melon seeds, and other plants. In 1737 Collinson sent a package of seeds for Thomas Penn with a shipment of cuttings and seeds to John Bartram and asked his "Dear Friend John" to deliver them with the instructions to "Dress thy self Neatly in thy Best Habits & wait on him for them for I have in a pticular manner Recommended thee to Him—I have Desired

Him to show thee the Natural History of South Carolina in Eight Books, finely Colour'd to the Life."

Collinson was a businessman and collector. He lived in London and had a country house outside of the city called Mill Hill where he experimented with American plants that Bartram and other collectors sent him. He wrote letters to a large group of correspondents linking them with each other through his good will and curiosity. According to Alan Armstrong, he stood at his shipping desk in his fabric shop in London scratching the letters out between customers and work. Over 750 of his letters survive. His export business to the British colonies was lucrative until the Revolution. He encouraged Benjamin Franklin in his experiments with electricity and was an advocate for John Bartram and his explorations for American plants. Through his efforts Bartram's plants were matched with willing patrons and dispatched to the large gardens on country estates. He introduced forty new plants to English gardens through Bartram and sent to American gardens pear scions, peach stones, melon seeds, and rhubarb.

In the morning my husband walks past the Rodin Museum over the landscape of Springettsbury down the long sidewalk to the school where he teaches. It's a Quaker school, and I once attended one of the weekly Wednesday meetings for worship there. I understand Thomas Penn's reluctance to continue in his father's faith. The meeting house is bare and formal. The benches descend to the center where the facing benches line the wall. My son finds the meeting long and silent. When someone does speak it seems less the voice of God and more the collective voice of discontent. I prefer the elaborate, expensive gold of our St. Francis Xavier's down the street, where the priests reassure me that although I'm a sinner and this world is vanishing, I can reap my rewards in the next.

Thomas Penn wanted his rewards here—after all, his father had worked hard for the bounty that his sons inherited. Penn imported his deer for the first deer park in the colonies, preferring English "fallow deer" to Pennsylvania deer. He put the English deer in a fenced wood east of the house and extended their yard to a stream and marsh that have disappeared now. He hired a huntsman. The deer liked the brush by the swamp and they mingled with Penn's pheasants and wild turkeys that lived there, too.

Peter Kalm, a Swedish botanist and traveler, came to Philadelphia in 1748. He was sent to the colonies by the Swedish Academy of Natural Sciences to collect specimens and write descriptions of plants, animals, and minerals of the New World. He described the native deer: "The thick forests of America contain numerous stags; they do not seem to be a different species from the European stags."

He examines a "hind that was caught when it was very small" and tamed by an Englishman who sold stags to people in Philadelphia, who then sent them "as curiosities to other places."

"The color of its whole body," he writes, "was a dirty reddish brown, the belly and the under side of the tail excepted, which were white; the ears were gray, the head, toward the nose, was very narrow, but upon the whole the creature looked slim and trim."

William Penn had planted a vineyard at Fairmount and employed a Frenchman, Andre Doz, to grow his grapes. Thomas started his vineyard with cuttings sent by Peter Collinson.

His father wrote: "The Great Red Grape (now ripe) called by Ignorance the Fox Grape (because of the Relish it hath with unskillful palates) is in itself an extraordinary grape, and by Art, doubtles may be cultivated to an excellent Wine, if not so sweet, yet little inferior to the Frontenack, as it is not much unlike in taste, ruddiness set aside, which in such things, as well as mankind, differs the case much."

William Penn believed in the miracle of a vineyard, but the native grapes were never satisfactory in their transformations. He wanted to make wonderful wine in his new colony, just as he wanted to design an efficient and beautiful city and an estate at Pennsbury that employed conservation. Thomas Penn's success was no greater than his father's. The wine was bitter and the vines withered. Or did they?

Some accounts report that James Alexander grew delicious grapes. He discovered a hybrid vine near the swampy edge of the Schuylkill River near William Penn's original vineyards. It's called the Alexander grape now and is a cross between an unidentified native and a vinifera vine.

Alexander sold seeds and plants along with working as Penn's gardener, and probably grew vegetables at Springettsbury. His seeds included peas, beans, onions, carrots, parsnips, radish, lettuce, celery, broccoli, white endive, marjoram, and cauliflower. Penn instructed Alexander to plant berries and fruits, including gooseberries and strawberries, near the greenhouse. He planted peaches and cherries and fig trees. When Thomas Penn was in London, Alexander sent carefully packed boxes of plants wrapped in bog moss and seeds in paper to Penn and some of his friends.

Penn's instructions to Alexander for a box of plants for the king are to fill the box with anything that is beautiful. In a letter written on April 2, 1755, Alexander explains that no one can be trusted "except John Bartram" for assistance in securing plants for English customers. Bartram, though, "has commonly demands for more that he can grow and therefore could not be prevailed on to part with such without a great price." Alexander tells Penn that he's hired a gardener to help with his business.

John Bartram writes to Peter Collinson in 1756 that "I cant imagine how or after what manner or with what James alexander fills so many boxes but this I know he frequents the market & discourses with all the people . . . when I go to gather seeds where I used to find them the people near where they grow will not let me have them but tell me thay will gather them all to send to London." Alexander was interested in agricultural practices as well as in the solar system and architecture. He became a member of the American Philosophical Society and was part of the committee to observe the transit of Venus. One visitor to Springettsbury remarked about his "curious Thermometer of spirits and mercury" in the greenhouse. He had an orrery and a "solar microscope."

Lewis Evans, a cartographer who mapped the land northwest of Philadelphia, described Alexander in 1753 as "very skill'd in every thing useful as well as curious relating to the politer, as well as more vulgar Culture in our plantations & gardens."

Thomas Penn left Philadelphia in 1741 and did not see Springettsbury again. He married Juliana Fermor, a wealthy woman who was not adventuresome and preferred London to a distant and dangerous place. She was much younger than he was and came from a powerful family. Penn died in 1775 in England. His family managed his property until 1787, renting some sections of the estate to tenants and opening others to the public. As late as the mid-eighteenth century travelers commented on the two-mile vista, "pretty pleasure garden," graveled walks bordered with shrubs and evergreens, "small wilderness" groves, a "neat little park though without deer," and spruce hedges cut into figures, "the most agreeable variety."

Deborah Logan, the wife of George Logan, grandson of James Logan, William Penn's manager of the colony and friend of John Bartram, wrote in her diary in 1815 on September 27: "Passing one day by the old manor of Springetsbury, I greatly desired to stop and look at the remains of the garden, which I had often frequented when a girl. The little greenhouse is now a ruin. In my youth an aloe was in flower, and crowds flocked out of town every fine day for many weeks to see the curiosity."

"Some of the fine labyrinths and hedges," she writes, "broke loose from the restraint of the sheers and, grown up behind the greenhouse, form a dark grove of evergreens. Broom and some other European plants still grow wild . . . (And I think it was the prettiest old-fashioned garden that I was ever in.)"

In 1826 she writes about the garden again after reading a letter from James Logan to John Penn in March 1742

with a Paragraph to Mrs Freame his Sister, who had just left this country with her Bro Thomas, and gives her an account of the increasing beauty of the Green house at Springetsbury which she had built and stocked with plants during her residence in the country, and speaks of the loneliness of the place without the agreeable company that was want to be assembled there.—The Gardens at Springets-bury were in full beauty in my youth, and were really very agreeable after the old fashion with Parterres, Gravelled walks, a Labyrinth of Horn-beam and a little wilderness—And the Green house, under the Superintendence of Old Virgil the Gardener, produced a flowering Aloe which almost half the town went to see, produced a comfortable Revenue to the old man—Soon after the house was burnt down by accident; and now quantities of the yellow Blossoms of Broom in spring time mark the place . . . "where once the gardens smiled."

The manor house burned in 1794, and the land was sold to Robert Morris three years later. A detail of a city map drawn in 1798 shows no buildings standing in the swatch of field and woods that was once Springettsbury.

Yesterday I walked home from my son's school in the cold morning air, all the light washed now with frost.

As I walked down the Parkway I thought about the hermit crab I know is buried in the churchyard of the cathedral. And the painted parrot and other small animals buried here by children from Graham's school. The green and brown ribbed shell of the hermit crab, the chartreuse and turquoise feathers of the parrot. Graham took me there once and searched the scuffed ground under a tall white pine for signs of the grave.

"Here it is," he said.

We examined the fallen leaves, the dark color of the soil. "It's a good place to be," I said.

I passed a cluster of shiny starlings pecking at crumbs. A flock of pigeons scattered into the air. The leaves of the sycamore had fallen, their large brown shapes disintegrating with pieces of paper and plastic cups and candy wrappers that cover the sharp cold blades of grass.

Soon I reached the dirt path by the Youth Study Center, the children's prison. I was walking near the ghost of the house at Springettsbury. The large house may have stood in the footprint of the concrete of the building. Five men camped out against the walls. They've wrapped their bodies in blankets and plastic bags. One man sleeps on a mattress. Above him the shiny whorls of razor wire glinted in the cold light.

Near us lay the neatly graveled paths and clever topiary, the painted fences and flowers, the goldfish pond. This time of year, though, everything would be eclipsed by the view of the wide shallow river across the fields and through the thickets. You could see the shimmer of the water, a view travelers have remarked about for many years.

I've been here long enough to know that the river washes itself clean. I imagined it as I walked, the curve above the boathouses clotted with bottles and plastic bags, logs and shiny foil, becoming perfectly clear.

I walked past people hurrying to their occupations, a man in a brown coat and polished black shoes, a briefcase slung over his shoulder, a woman pushing two little girls in a double stroller fast past me on the pavement once I rounded the corner and headed north.

I wondered about vanished lives. The sifting and interring of the past, all that accumulation gone, turned over, invisible in the concrete wall of an almost present place. Neighborhoods in the city have disappeared under corporate buildings, just as the landscape of marsh and stream is almost no longer here. I listened to a woman talk about her neighborhood at a conference on Friday at the Historical Society. She said she and her neighbors meet once a year to commemorate several blocks of streets where they once lived in West Philadelphia called Black Bottom.

In the 1950s and '60s the houses and gardens of the African American neighborhood were swallowed by the University of Pennsylvania and Drexel University and demolished. "We preserve it," she said, "by remembering."

It seemed important to several people that they had ancestors who came over on the *Mayflower*. They could trace who they were all the way back to when their ancestors stepped off their cramped boats and started a new life here. These people had lived six or seven decades. They were sure of the value of the past, the importance of preserving something they called "the built environment."

I don't know the details of my historic past. My family kept no record of their travels. No one wrote anything down. My ancestors left Canada or Ireland alone when they were only a few years older than my son. They left small farms where the pigs slept in the other room. No one has bothered to trace our past. My grandmothers didn't talk about it.

Thomas Penn's letters are bound in leather volumes in the Historical Society. I read the small script standing over the library table and lean against the crumbling edge of the leather book. The letters are attached to the huge pages and to read the backs I flip the page over carefully. Here's one from January 1739 that instructs Penn's agent and friend, Richard Hockley, to buy slaves for him in "Charles Town" and to get a present for his sister.

"Dear Dick," he writes, "I sent you abroad to make an acquantance with the best People in Carolina." He also wants a "white servant who has been used to wait on a gentleman" and "two Boys and a Girl." One of the boys will be a carpenter and the other will be "used" in the house, and the girl will be for "common house use." Hockley replies in April 1740 that he has found "three fine young slaves" but they were expensive because the "assembly have made an Act lately though not yet in force, in order to prevent the Importation of such great quantities of Slaves."

I'm trying to find out more about the men and women who took care of Penn's house and his greenhouse, his hornbeam labyrinth and his topiary. Several sources tell me that in 1733 Virgil Warder was sold to Thomas Penn, and he lived until he was very old. Penn's family paid him and his wife Susannah a pension to take care of the house after Thomas Penn died in England. They lived in the kitchen wing of the house. One source states that "Susannah Warden, formerly the wife of Virgil Warden," died in 1809 "in her 109th year." Virgil Warder was born in Bucks County, Pennsylvania, and sold by Joseph Warder. So he was born into slavery. It's not clear from the documents whether he was a free man at his death in 1782 or '83.

Other accounts tell me that James Alexander managed the property and lived in the house with his wife Anne Ellis and four sons until his death in 1778. Anne and one of his sons died before him. Alexander's possessions at his death were a small collection of books, including Pope's *Works*, Grew's *Anatomy of Plants*, and *Indian Nations* in two volumes. He also owned a "Tallascope," chests, drawers, bags of seed, and fourteen beehives.

Alexander sent a bill to Penn in February 1741 listing "sundry charges on the Account" of a man known only as Sam. Was he one of the men Richard Hockley bought in South Carolina in 1740? And was Susannah the "girl to be used in the house"?

Sam gets sick for three weeks, and expenses include a nurse and "nesesarys for Sam." Alexander charges Penn for food and reimbursement for "three weeks of his sickness" and money for rum, wine, and spices for the burial and attendance "2 days and a night" on the body. Diana is paid for "washing and dressing him when dead." He lists the cost of a coffin, grave, and burying ground. One of the items is for shaving Sam after his death.

When I run on the edge of the baseball fields I can see where the stream once cut through the land at Springettsbury in the soggy indentations near the Parkway. Under the field is the memory of the stream cutting through the small woodland to the river.

# 5. Lemons

ONCE THERE WAS A LARGE GREENHOUSE near us on Lemon Hill, the high flat bluff overlooking the river, where Henry Pratt grew all sorts of exotic citrus trees not far from Thomas Penn's greenhouse. This morning I walked up the stone steps past the dry fountain through the woods and past the cream-colored house to the fields. I can't name the old trees surrounding the house, but others I know— a two-story rhododendron, a ginkgo as tall as any tree I've seen on this coast, and beeches with broad trunks and smooth gray skin and rippled roots.

I picked up a seed husk under one of the tall trees. I hold it in my hand. This hull is tiny, the size of a fingertip, and split open into an empty flower. Rough light brown, four petals curved in, ridged like wood, the outside spiky with furry thorns. When I hold the seed husk in my hand it sits in the center like a jewel. Harmless, opened, seed dispersed, chewed up by a squirrel, or buried, squashed by a foot, digested into a chipmunk's cells.

Horse chestnut. Maybe. A spiny husk fallen on the grass at Lemon Hill. It's small, too small I think to be a horse chestnut, poisonous cousin of the European chestnut, the sweet roasted chestnuts of New York street corners.

The tree that dropped the seed is perhaps three hundred years old on a hill that was cultivated almost two hundred years before the city bought the property in 1855 as part of the park system, a protection for the drinking water in the river below the cliff.

I try to imagine the slope of the river where it once fell over rapids to its confluence with the Delaware. I try to see the sweep of hill to where I write now, a gradual incline up from the bank to a place called

The Hills by Robert Morris, just over the rise from our house, where William Penn grew grapes on a bluff above the river.

I've been finding out some things about Lemon Hill. I spent a morning last week in the Horticultural Society library fingering the old pages of a pamphlet and a privately printed book.

The librarian brought me the books in boxes. The bookbinder had printed a card just inside the boxes explaining what she had done to prolong the life of the pages. They were leathery and spotted with brown, the ink on both documents brown too. Or do I just remember it as brown?

The pamphlet was a catalog "of Splendid and Rare Green House and Hot House Plants: To Be Sold by Auction, at Lemon Hill, Formerly the Seat of the Late Henry Pratt, Deceased, on Tuesday, the 5th day of June, 1838, and to be continued Daily Till Completed, By D. & C. A. Hill, Auctioneers."

The catalog was fifty-nine pages, and I could hold it in my hands like a concert program. It was filled with exotics. There were four pages of citrus fruits I could only imagine: St. Helena lemon, median lemon, variegated orange, lemon bergamot, sweet orange, *Citrus aurantium*, myrtle orange, and porcupine orange. I thought of the greenhouses crowded with the other magical trees and fine-leaved plants and bright, hot flowers listed in the catalog: coxcomb, coral tree, Madagascar periwinkle, purple dragon tree, *Ficus religiosa*, worshipful poplar leaved, bramble rose, stripe-leaved aloe, rush-leaved broom, fine-flowering sage, *Coffea arabica*, and Bengal fig.

In a little more than ten years all the greenhouses, already emptied of their fragrant fruit and startling plants, would be gone. The elaborate gardens of Mr. Pratt where Philadelphians could come and stroll and admire were almost not here at all:

at the end of this time, by neglect, by fire, and by wanton destruction, this place, the abode of a once princely luxury, had fallen into ruin;

where beautiful hot-houses filled with rare exotics overlooked the river, only falling walls blackened by fire remained—the shrubbery had been destroyed—the little bark grotto over the spring, and the shady summer houses had decayed, and the ponds filled with the gold fish had become loathsome with slime; only the grand old tulip trees remained, and the pines, which stood as they still stand today, silent sentinels around the deserted mansion, where the great financier, whose guests were Washington and Franklin and Jefferson, held his Republican Court.

Robert Morris, often called the financier of the American Revolution, owned the land, part of the original acres of Springettsbury, before and after the Revolution. So says my source, the anonymous narrator of the small book I held in my hand as I sat at the clean wood table in the Horticultural Society's library. Morris built a house in 1770 that was burned by the British and rebuilt after the Revolution. The grounds were "planned on a large scale, the gardens and walks are extensive, and the villa situated on an eminence, has a commanding prospect down the Schuylkill." The estate also had a very large greenhouse with lemon trees.

In 1799 Morris, bankrupt, sold the land and the few buildings that still stood at the estate to Mr. Pratt, who owned the land for quite a long time. At his death the dismantling of the property began. The greenhouses were stripped, and the next owner, Isaac S. Loyd, bought the land, 42 acres and 93 perches of ground between the railroad and the Schuylkill, for $225,000 in 1836. In 1843 Thomas Cope, a prominent businessman, the librarian tells me, bought the property for the city. For many years there were attempts to make the land the first section of a city park to protect the drinking water in the Schuylkill. It was just outside the city limits at this time, and council members proposed a cemetery.

Andrew Jackson Downing described the gardens in the early 1820s in his book *A Treatise on the Theory and Practice of Landscape Gardening*:

> Lemon Hill . . . was, 20 years ago, the most perfect specimen of the geometric mode in America, and since its destruction by the extension of the city, a few years since, there is nothing comparable with it, in that style, among us. All the symmetry, uniformity, and high art of the old school, were displayed here in artificial plantations, formal gardens with trellises, grottoes, spring-houses, temples, statues, and vases, with numerous ponds of water, jets-d'eau, and other waterworks, parterres and an extensive range of hot houses. The effect of this garden was brilliant and striking; its position on the lovely banks of the Schuylkill, admirable; and its liberal proprietor, Mr. Pratt, by opening it freely to the public, greatly increased the popular taste in the neighborhood of that city.

I've been down to the river this morning to the place where I can see the house on Lemon Hill through the silhouettes of small trees that were not there when Thomas Cope bought the property. I can trace the outline of the wide, curving windows that face the river, and beyond the river a highway that cuts through the parkland on the other side, and beyond the highway the railroad, its towers poking up into the milky sky. We live almost on the edge of the original acres. They're just down the street. I can see where the lawn extended down the bluff and the fields bordered the reservoir where the art museum now commands the view.

I've been in the house. I've seen the curved doors and the perfectly oval rooms, the wood fashioned by shipbuilders. I've heard about the parties that Pratt had in the summer, all the doors thrown open to the breeze off the river carrying the scent of the flowering trees. I've walked on the dark green floors and padded over the rush mats, stood at the edge of the expensive green carpet in the drawing room where the guests would play cards at night as the women protected their waxy makeup from the heat of the candle with a little wooden plate on a stand. Their faces, the guide told me, had been disfigured by smallpox so they filled in the scars with white wax.

I've seen the river from the curved shining windows and imagined that I was standing on the porch at dusk as the bats consumed their evening meal.

Our guide brought her children up in the house built in 1799 in an apartment on the ground floor where Mr. Pratt had his kitchen. Her husband was a mounted officer in Fairmount Park, and she watched as the neighborhood changed around the hill.

"It was bad in the '80s with drugs," she said. She's painted tiny lemons on small clear glasses for the gift shop.

My author assures me that he felt like he owned Lemon Hill when he examined it in 1855. After all, it was given to the city by Cope, and finally, after several years, the city declared the property a park to be called Fairmount Park. It was the first portion of a very large city park that would spread up the Schuylkill and along the Wissahickon.

What the author wanted was this: "We have thus traced to its legal conclusion, the history of a small portion of the greater design, now become a necessity, of enclosing a sufficient portion of both sides of the Schuylkill river above the dam, to preserve the water from contamination, and secure at the same time, in the most eligible spot near the city, a pleasure-ground commensurate with the demands of its crowded population."

The city was ready to evict the tenants on the property, but the tenants had other ideas. They had boarded up the gate, put up no trespassing signs, built "huge structures of wood" and were "engaged with their crops" on the afternoon our author visited. They had built an ice house and a brick boat house on the river. He went up to the hill about this time of year, November, in the long fall he calls Indian

Summer, ripe, glowing, warm. Maples blazed red. Giant tulip trees spread their gold leaves on the hill suspended between two water-works. He mourns the ruined summer houses and admires the view of the river.

"Parks," he writes, quoting Lord Chatham, "are the lungs of the city." The cost of the park would be twenty-five cents per person, he estimates. "We want the great broad avenue of pure air to flow through our city."

When I walk along the Parkway past the art museum, through the azalea garden and up the slope to Lemon Hill, I follow the lungs of the city. The great nineteenth-century landscape designers like Frederick Law Olmsted saw their newly green creations as breathing life into the industrial cities of the late 1800s. These places had lost most of their breathing space to factories and crowded rows of houses where there had once been small parks and backyard gardens.

I walk toward Lemon Hill under sycamore trees planted a hundred years ago, their mottled green and brown bark shining in the clear, low light of November. An arborist who came to look at our trees told me that Penn loved sycamore trees. He had them planted all over his new city. They grew relatively quickly, and they could be hacked back for firewood and would grow again. Settlers planted them near springhouses to keep the water cool. They'll take a little wet on their feet. They can grow three sets of leaves in a season, dropping one after the other in response to a dry year. After two years of drought several have died, though, and now only the place where their roots hugged the ground is left, crunched down to chips, a blank reddish circle on the grass. It will take up to five years to tell how the drought has affected some trees. The sycamores looked halfhearted all summer.

The average life of street trees in a city is ten years so I feel rich when I walk under the trees on Lemon Hill. Often they're full of birds. If I'm lucky I'll see hawks or a peregrine falcon. On Lemon Hill this morning I stood on the pavilion perched on the edge of the cliff that ends at the road. I could see the river and the railroad and the streaming cars. I saw where the falcons nest on the cliffs along the river.

Today the sycamores are bare and bruised green and white. Their large thick limbs sway this way and that against the sky that has no color really, no taste, no memory. I'll never see St. Helena lemons or porcupine oranges growing in the greenhouses on the hill.

Yesterday I moved my small orange tree inside. Now it sits just near the sliding doors in my bedroom. Soon all the small hard green fruit will turn orange. I've never owned a citrus tree before. This one is a gift from George, our neighbor. I love the shiny leaves and gnarled trunk and the hard little green fruit on the end of each branch. I like watching the blossoms turn to fruit and then the fruit ripen and drop. The fruit is sweet and tangy and has the zip of a tangerine.

# 6. Wild Grasses

I'M TAKING STOCK of my surroundings on this warm fall afternoon—a wild thicket grown up at the end of the street, a slope that once led to the river and hill where William Penn had his vineyard with bitter grapes. The deck garden is swept clean by rain, a persistent Carolina chickadee comes again and again to the empty feeder. Monarchs float their way south, a dazzling dragonfly with spotted wings buzzes over my head in the community garden. Children in their red and blue uniforms cascade onto the sidewalk, Father Georges laughs about something, the smell of roasting chickens salts the air.

Cornstalks, baby popcorn dry and yellow in their pot, the tomatoes long gone, basil cut down to nubs.

Now Father Georges comes by the house as I fiddle in the garden and says, "You should join the ladies who do the flowers in church."

"Maybe I will."

I'm trying to will myself into wilderness this morning. There's a braided delta at the mouth of the Schuylkill. Woolly mammoths dig their shiny horns into the muck. Look, there's a huge bird flying above the shaggy heads. Mastodons and caribou come to drink at the river. Hunters have not arrived on the scene, and no one dares plant a garden anywhere near here. The ocean miles away is frothy and cold. The estuary is a clean mix of salt pulled from the ocean and fresh water from the river. Fossils are curled somewhere near as we watch. I'm not sitting in a house in a row of houses. No empty barrels lie on the street. No one is hungry, not the child or the man or the woman at the corner asking for a dollar for breakfast. There is nothing to be envious of. The plumes of fierce birds shine dark black.

Spruce bristles in the clear November light. Moss uncurls on the hillsides. The river twists on a treeless expanse in all its cold glitter. This is almost the beginning, the ice barely gone. It's a new slate, here at the edge of the southern tip of the glacier. Earthworms wiggle in the newly warm soil. Soon everything will hum with life.

And then it won't be wilderness at all, will it? But a place where families clear the land for beans and corn, squash and pumpkins, vegetables from the south and the elaborate terraced gardens there. And sometimes they kill birds that are on their way north or south and fish baskets full of shad from the river on their way up to spawn. It's a wild river, not dammed or rerouted or bordered but still flowing into the braided delta, still shining, where thousands of birds gather. I'd call it a wilderness. There are elk and wolves. Sometimes the men hunt for animals and the women gather nuts and berries, very sweet. And presently peaches will be introduced by the men who come in ships from across the ocean, and then there will be orchards of these peaches and open fields burned clear of brush. If I set foot here now, here where the wide coastal plain, sandy and flat, abruptly meets the rock of the Piedmont, I'd still call it wilderness. The trees are towering. The fish are so plentiful in the river, I watch myself walk from one side to the other on their backs. So many birds fill the sky, I pull them down and into my mouth with a quick gesture. How could I know the land was once very cold and hardly anything lived here at all?

It won't take long for all this abundance to be whittled down into a place not called wilderness at all. And this is where it gets tricky. Because isn't it still a wilderness of sorts? The bones of the wilderness still there in the brooks flowing in pipes under the city, the soil that pokes up with its own history of the old wilderness soil, rerouted, recycled elements. I see it in the back patio between the flagstones or in the garden three blocks away where I heel in the mums and cover the ground with elm leaves. It pops up around the street trees and in the matted roots in the drains. A large expanse of rough grass grows along the river and in patches of parks carved out before the city filled itself in like a coloring book. And the birds still entertain us: a redstart miraculously bright orange and black on the bent stalk of a small dry sunflower, a red-tailed hawk flapping once, twice, three times above the tip of a giant tulip tree. It's enough to make me think I'm imagining everything else. And I could, if I were strong enough, rip the fabric of the city at the edge and peel it away to rocks that were there all the time. Wilderness just under the surface. Breathing its clear breath right into my face.

I often have this familiar feeling of disappearing—there's no one here—except the cardinal drinking water from the roof we can see from the second floor windows. A short burst of rain and then nothing. The cardinal's wet from the rain and sipping careful sips from the pool on the black rubber roof. The sky's white, the elm leaves hang perfectly still—sparrows chirp in their puddles on the street. The bricks of our neighbor's house continue to hold themselves up as they have for a century. Imperfect, irregular, practical. The white sky could be an ocean or a lake or the luminous inside of a shell.

The elms rustle their leaves and down the street the maple follows suit. Twigs and branches wiggle too, a green reminder of the forest that stretches all the way along the river from here in one fashion or another to the far north, a green doorway to wilderness.

# 7. Tulip Tree

IF YOU WANTED TO, you could walk from our house northwest along the Schuylkill to the Wissahickon, a tributary of the wide, tidal river. It's one of the green arms of Fairmount Park, the extensive park nineteenth-century travelers called "Philadelphia's Garden." Lemon Hill was the first part of the park, bought to preserve the purity of the river water. Our trees are part of the park, too, the spiritual descendants of the original woods.

The park has old roads, crumbling asphalt, low branches where birds, sparrows perhaps, make their nests. The sparrows sit in the branches as you pass down into the deep woods, severing spider webs as you walk closer to the river. These are old woods, steep embankments, the broken backs of roads. In summer there's a crescendo of insect song. Explosions of wings near the water. You can't hear traffic or laughter. Carriages passed over the river on a mossy stone bridge a hundred years ago.

Thirty mills once lined the Wissahickon, houses, barns, a landscape of industry. The first mill was built in 1683, and they multiplied in the eighteenth century. In the 1800s the city annexed the creeks that flowed into the Schuylkill to protect the water supply drawn from the river. We still drink the waters of the Schuylkill and the Wissahickon. You can tell how cold the river is as the water flows out of the tap. In the winter the water is chilled, sometimes flowing from the river covered with ice; in summer, the water won't get cold no matter how long you let it run. The shallow river is tepid under the hot July sun.

Since 1900, the forest along the Wissahickon has returned, a forest of beech, large round trunks light and cool to the touch, the tatters of thin leaves still fluttering in winter, tulip trees with exotic blossoms—yellow and light green—that crush under your feet in spring, and oak, and feathery hemlock.

A few days ago we hiked along Wissahickon Creek. I'd been thinking about Edgar Allan Poe. He lived around the corner from us on Fairmont Avenue, called Coates Street then. One of his biographers tells me that he was despondent during his young wife's long illness, but on good days he would take a picnic to the park near here and they would sit in the warm fall sunshine on the riverbank. Sometimes he walked with friends around to the reservoir constructed on the hill overlooking the falls on the Schuylkill.

Poe wrote a short piece called "Morning on the Wissahiccon" in 1843 describing the charms of the river. He floated through the narrow cliffs and still pools looking up into the tall tulip trees. He fell asleep. At one point he saw an elk. He was pleased that he was in a wilderness of a sort, until he saw the elk's keeper scatter food to lure the elk back home to a villa in the woods. Poe writes: "Indeed, in America generally, the traveler who would behold the finest landscapes, must seek them not by the railroad, nor by the steamboat, nor by the stage-coach, nor in his private carriage, nor yet even on horseback—but on foot."

I've learned that he made $800 a year, twice the money a laborer would make and about the same as a ship carpenter. When Poe lived around the corner there were 1,673 private bathtubs in the center of the city. You could pay $7.50 for a water hydrant in front of your house. Water for a bathtub was $4 extra.

We took the train past the houses that had bathtubs in Poe's time through the rubble of the north where buildings were collapsing all summer, a soggy few months eating at the roofs where trees had already invaded vacant rooms. Street after street missing blocks of houses like gaps in teeth, built quick and close at the turn of the twentieth century, connected to the center of the city first by trolley and then car. And the empty factories and schools, their windows broken in a pattern of punched holes. Fields of junk cars glimmered in the sun, a green square here and there, a small garden wedged between two houses, sunflowers on the edge of a parking lot. Soon we were climbing into Mt. Airy and Chestnut Hill and their large houses, some crumbling like those in north Philadelphia, others gleaming with new paint and large trees and big yards. Here the houses are built of native stone, Wissahickon schist—gray, textured chunks of rock with flecks of shining mica fitted together to form villas and cottages, walls and garden terraces in the early 1900s.

We got off the train at Highland Station and walked along a road past large houses to a lane that dropped to the river. Once we reached the Wissahickon we were surprised. It smelled wild. We walked the east side on a narrow trail along the steep bank.

For a moment we couldn't remember where we were: the leaves falling one by one in a yellow blur, rhododendron edging into the path, the impossible height of the tulip trees and beech trees filling the sky above us.

Graham wobbled on the slippery rocks and I counted crackers in the plastic container in my backpack. It was astonishing to be here, no whisper of cars, the steady churn of the water as it rushed and then slowed and then rushed on its way to the ocean.

When we crossed the river to an old road called Forbidden Drive we were almost halfway to the mouth where the creek meets the Schuylkill. There's an inn here that was built in 1850, a white wooden building called the Valley Green Inn. At one time there were several inns near the Wissahickon.

"It's too hot in there," Graham said.

"Do you have a reservation?" a young woman with a starched white shirt and black skirt asked.

"No," we said, wondering why we didn't pack a lunch before we set out in the morning. Scott bought popcorn and lemonade and turned down the hot dogs for cookies at the snack stand outside. We sat on a bench watching the water, wide and shallow, filled with ducks and geese splashing and gobbling bread and chattering.

I leaned back against the bench and tried to think soothing thoughts. I was not serene. I was not Edgar Allan Poe. I was not even a very good mother. After all, my child was tired and hungry, my husband out of sorts (he confessed later that his back hurt), and we still had three miles to walk and a train to catch or a long walk back.

Like the settlers who answered Penn's advertisements and made the journey across the Atlantic in their small boats, I've landed in a foreign landscape. I don't have the vocabulary to understand it. There's no spiritual significance in the land for me.

I have no connections here, no friends or relations, my history doesn't touch this creek or this river, their patch of ground in the mid-Atlantic. When my uncle moved to Pennsylvania it was as if he had emigrated to a foreign country. We didn't see him for years. And then he moved even farther away to Delaware.

My husband and my son share a connection to this part of the country. Scott's mother and father grew up near the Delaware River in Trenton and Somerville. This is the place where his ancestors landed at the end of their journeys from their small towns in Germany or England or Ireland. To Scott the landscape is familiar. Two of his aunts still live near here.

But I feel no tug of remembrance about the trees in the woods— too tall, the vegetation—too lush, the shape of the hills—perhaps like England? My landscape is the pasture, the house on the pasture, naked, familiar, a place where once were cows. Pastoral subdivided in any number of ways, Connecticut fields sold to lots first large then small. My woods bounded the fields. They were filled with second growth and crumbling houses of farmers who had moved west. When we went into the woods we touched the past; we scrambled around the cellar holes and boarded windows of someone who once farmed the land where our houses and bikes and cars and swing sets stood. Our parents usually knew who the farmers were. Sometimes we thought the old houses were haunted.

I've never lived in a place that hasn't been cut up, plowed over, paved, or rearranged in some way or another. But usually I knew what had been there before. I have to unearth the geography of this city. Sift myself down through the layers of what was once here and still resides in the earth under the house where we sleep and our son grows taller every day. I don't understand the light, the way fall is not fall but a long stretch of September into winter, the flat shine of the river, the absence of night.

Perhaps if I learn the history and the geography, the particulars of this place, I too can start to inhabit my life here and the woods will begin to have their own significance.

There was something strangely pleasant about being in that stretch of woods between one rushing road and the next, very quiet, eating first one popcorn kernel and then the next, sipping the cold bottled lemonade, my son's head on my shoulder, my husband flipping cookies into a Tupperware of now-vanished peanut butter cookies. These trees had survived. Some were large enough, we thought, to be two hundred years old. There were numerous deer, some very large in the woods, and there was the season, fall coming down all around us in its gold and yellow splendor. Rhododendrons as tall as I am, dark green ferns, stiff and important on the bank, chickadees arguing in the branches of the smaller trees, and those tall straight tulip trees reaching up to the clear sky.

On the road once more we coaxed Graham along with the thought of a snack at the end.

"Look," I said, "you still have popcorn left and two Oreo cookies. When we get the train you can eat them, won't that be fun?"

All along the creek people were fishing. A man in green waders flicked his green line above his head and let it touch lightly on the cool river; a man and a woman standing close together on the bank held their poles just above the water's edge.

"Are there caves?" Graham asked.

"You mean like the Hardy boys?"

We pulled him close when riders came by on bikes or horses, flying up the trail, kicking the gravel and dust on the road that had been constructed between 1823 and 1856. Little piles of mossy stones curved in balustrades on the steep banks, artifice of the road builders.

I was thinking about Poe again as we passed a quiet place above an old dam where he could have floated in his "skiff," the sun hot on his face, thinking about beauty. I was trying to think about beauty but my son was complaining and my husband accused me of monosyllabic answers. Graham started to repeat a word over and over again. We had two miles to go.

We were above the river and could see the yellow leaves of the oaks, beeches, and the yellow leaves of the tulip trees drift down to the shining stream, green where it was slow, yellow and glittering where it was fast. Soon we were at the end of the old road and there was music and the hum of the highway above us. Two men were on the bank of the river below us, one playing a large kettle drum, the other hitting a bamboo pole with a stick. They had a fire ready to light and faced each other on the edge of the swirling creek.

We took the last mile slowly and fought our way along the narrow paved trail, dodging bikers. At one point I stopped to give Graham some water and a cookie. We looked toward the river and saw a muskrat in the shallows. He swam on the surface and dipped under to swim fast along the sandy bottom of the creek riled with the motion of the water. I had never seen a muskrat before. He was smooth and light brown and compact.

The water was shallow and I could see the waves of sand under the muskrat's body as he slid, soft and swift, almost the same color as the warm brown of the bottom. I remembered wading in the brook behind our house when I was Graham's age. I could feel the sandy bottom of the creek, the cool water silky on my toes.

# 8. Catalpa

MY FEET COULD BE BARE padding along the trodden path that winds under sycamores one hundred years old. I'm walking along the slope of Springettsbury where the land levels off toward the river. As I walk the dirt path I concentrate on the color of the mud, how cold it would feel on my feet, and what it would be like to lie there, my cheek pressed against the cold dirt, the city distracted by itself all around me.

The starlings like it here, too. I startle a small bird who shimmers in iridescent feathers in the early light. I'm all shimmer here in the city as the season turns to late fall. Men curl in blankets and coats along the benches, their heads hidden in sweaters or hats pulled low.

My path takes me toward the river. The air is clean, wind cool, sunlight warms my bones. I let the noise and litter bounce off me like spray.

Near the Philadelphia Museum of Art the Schuylkill River nudges into the green lawn and the base of the nineteenth-century waterworks where an elaborate garden once meandered along the river and up the steep slopes to a reservoir on the top of Fair Mount. William Penn's vineyard, once here, vanished under the waters of the river pumped up to the hill, and then the glittering lake vanished too under the stone of the art museum. Against the dark rock cliff below the reservoir in the rocks of the Piedmont was a white wooden statue of a river nymph holding a bittern on her shoulder carved by William Rush, an artist who learned his trade carving figureheads.

Travelers in the early 1800s were delighted with fountains that spewed water over mythical figures and the silent cascade of the water in the pump houses moving over the miraculous machines. They wandered through the garden and climbed the cliffs on stone bridges fancy with ironwork. Once at the top, they saw the river spreading out below them, decorated with arching trees and the lawns of large estates, built by the rich escaping the summer heat and the pestilence of Philadelphia during mosquito season.

I can imagine the city years ago at that time of year, full of swamps on the outskirts and open rain barrels and sewers in the center into which people threw rotting carcasses and spoiled fruits. The air was thick with mosquitoes. Mothers worried about their children's health as another yellow fever epidemic swept through the neighborhoods. The first waterworks was built after the yellow fever epidemic of 1793. William Rush's statue was placed outside the waterworks, a small neoclassical building in Centre Square, spewing water into the humid air. When the new waterworks was built at Fair Mount the statue was transported to the base of the dark cliff below the reservoir. In 1872 Thomas Eakins painted *William Rush Carving His Allegorical Figure of the Schuylkill River.* By that time the wooden statue had crumbled, and Eakins used a bronze cast of the carving. The model in the Eakins work is luminous, her body glowing with the light that comes from an unknown source into the artist's studio.

I went to an exhibit not long ago of Thomas Eakins's work. I discovered that he grew elephant ears in his tiny backyard. The same large version of *Colocasia esculenta* we grow in the pot on our patio, bent down now—the long season of exuberance just about at an end.

I liked it that he lived a few streets away from our house for most of his life. I studied the small photographs of his house and his wife and his students and his cat and monkey. The one I studied the longest was of his backyard on Mt. Vernon Street in the late 1890s, a backyard like ours with a raised bed filled with elephant ears. There's a wooden chair and pots of ferns. His wife is holding their pet monkey's paw, and two cats peer at the photographer.

He took pictures of children and adults posed on his roof for the painting *Mending the Nets* and transferred their pose to oil. The backyard is full of dappled light, silver in the old photograph.

The photographs record his wife's unvarnished face, sitting in their apartment when they were first married before they moved back into his family's large home, his sister sitting on the back steps of the house with her setter years before she died of typhoid. And the men and boys by the river, all silver and naked like gods.

His wife, Susan Macdowell Eakins, was a painter, too. She was Eakins's student at the Pennsylvania Academy of the Fine Arts. She said that "his teaching crushed her for a while."

By the time Eakins was painting his darkly beautiful painting of a woman posing for Rush, the garden at the waterworks was quite large and extended around the reservoir and along the river. Rustic gazebos of rough branches perched on the cliff and a large hotel served drinks by the river.

Frances Trollope praised the waterworks when she visited Philadelphia in 1830:

> At a most beautiful point of the Schuylkill River the water has
> been forced up into a magnificent reservoir, ample and elevated
> enough to send it through the whole city. The vast yet simple machin-
> ery by which this is achieved is open to the public, who resort in such
> vast numbers to see it, that several evening stages run from Phila-
> delphia to Fair Mount for their accommodation . . . It is, in truth,
> one of the very prettiest spots the eye can look upon. A broad weir is
> thrown across the Schuylkill, which produces the sound and look of
> a cascade . . . The works themselves are enclosed in a simple but very
> handsome building of freestone, which has an extended front open-

ing upon a terrace, which overhangs the river: behind the building, and divided from it only by a lawn, rises a lofty wall of solid limestone rock, which has, at one or two points, been cut into, for the passage of the water into the noble reservoir above. From the crevices of this rock catalpa was everywhere pushing forth, covered with its beautiful blossom.

By midcentury the garden was as elegant as the pump houses spread out along the river. Steamboats docked at a weir on a spit of land that's now full of brush and skinny trees. The birds cluster there in a wild bit of territory just below the art museum. In the spring I hear red winged blackbirds. A heron nests here.

Once I saw a bittern on a bleached log in the shallow waters of the Schuylkill by the path where I walk every morning. I admired her bright yellow legs, her dark brown feathers. Sometimes a kingfisher darts from his perch in the thicket. He's all pearly flash and sharp beak as he dips into the water filled with weeds and logs and trash in the inlet near the museum.

In summer the thicket of oaks and willow brush throbs with the buzz saw creaking of cicadas. Very loud, almost louder than the rush of traffic on the highway on the west bank of the river. In the azalea garden the white plumes of hostas wave in the light breeze. Now sparrows sing their cheerful songs and a woman reads a book, her possessions spread around her on the bench. A man is going through the garbage bags in the parking lot near the river. Soon he starts throwing pieces of bread he's found to the ducks who scoot along the shore and gobble the crumbs up with their wide shiny beaks.

I walk back along the river to the waterworks. The catalpa trees are gone. No soft purple or yellow blooms, their throats creamy like foxgloves, bloom against the dark quarried rock.

# 9. Water Lilies

I MET TWO MEN FISHING in the shallow watery ghost of the waterworks garden this morning. They were dressed in green fishermen's clothes and had their licenses pinned to their shirts in plastic envelopes. It was sunny, and the wind was mild and from the north. They flicked their lines into the place where the water is midnight blue on a drawing I have of a plan for the Benjamin Franklin Parkway designed by Jacques Greber in 1919.

The Parkway was an ordered shining vision of paradise from the glittering blue pool in Logan Circle to the serpentine paths in the original waterworks garden. The art museum is the focal point of the Parkway. Three different types of trees march in green splendor toward the winged building on the hill. Tiny carts and carriages circle around the curved paths that lead to the building. On the steps Greber has drawn the silhouettes of slim shadowy figures.

The dark blue water cascades over the dam in white froth. Mixed plantings like an English shrubbery surround the museum and spread into the large garden that winds close to where the fishermen stand on the grassy edge of the lawn, tossing their lines into the still water of the inlet that flows almost up to the steps of the art museum. The drawing shows no tangly thicket or yellow water lilies at the narrow end of the inlet. Someone is cultivating this garden with great care.

"Used to be you could fish right over there on that land," the more talkative fisherman said. He nodded toward the thicket in front of us, beyond the inlet where the ferryboats used to pull up to the dock below the waterworks, women in silk dresses leaning out over the railing above the swirling waters.

The fishermen told me they catch crappies and smallmouth bass, yellow perch, and sometimes catfish and carp.

I asked them if there were still shad in the river, and the taller man told me he saw two upriver. He was reeling his line in, flicking it out to the water.

"They come up that ladder over there," and we all looked across the river to the other bank below the highway.

"It's not really a ladder, more like a channel that the fish swim through. I bet if you went over there right now there'd be a few in the rocks at the bottom."

You can't see up the river in the drawing, but I know there was a towpath and a canal on that side of the river.

A few days ago, he told me, "the shad were this big, everybody was catching them." And he held his hands about a foot and a half apart.

"About a week ago the fish like this," and the fisherman held his hands about six inches apart, "those little silver ones were coming through."

"Herring?"

"Yeah, that's them. You see them better when the tide's out, it's in now," he said.

I looked down at the swirling green water, foam in puffs on the surface, a mixture of salt and fresh water all the way up to the dam.

I read not long ago that *Alosa sapidissima*, or the "poor man's salmon," returns to the river of its birth to spawn. The prime breeding ground of shad is the Delaware River estuary. The Lenape used nets made of brush to catch the shad that swam up the Schuylkill, spawning in the little rills where the tributaries met the river. The Schuylkill was the best place to fish for shad in the 1700s until the dams were built upriver and at Fairmount in 1820.

I've been to the end of the town at the northwest corner along the river where shad once swam in countless numbers to spawn at Flatbrush Rock. I saw sloped-roof houses covered with wisteria, a row of trailers, and long lawns to the river.

Little streams flowed into the river. Graham pulled a cane of bamboo from a stand near a stream, separated the parts, put his hand in his mouth.

"You'd get swamped if you went out in a canoe," a blond man said. He was sitting on a dock.

"We just came in from water skiing."

Not far from here downriver the shad still spawn at Flatbush Rock. Once there were restaurants all along the river that served fish, catfish mostly.

Now the river is rich in birds. Two little blue herons fed in the shallows near the edge of the ghost of the old canal. I watched them fly up the river from the dam and choose their feeding places, lifting one leg and then another, cocking their heads to one side and then the other as they searched for fish. Sometimes when I walk by the river I watch the great blue heron, his gray feathers washed by the rain, his neck poised in a crook above the shallows where the other waterbirds wait for food. On the wire near the dam perched ten cormorants. One bird held her wings out to dry in the early sun, a magical clothesline of birds.

The city now pulls water from the river in a shallow upriver from the dam. You could put a canoe in there but I never see them on this stretch of water, just the impossibly slim boats pulling like water bugs on the surface.

Mallards and cormorants float in the river, all their soft feathers shining in the morning light. Their heads are electric green or glossy black. Sometimes the herons fly under the Girard Street Bridge, all intent on the upper reaches of the Schuylkill, or the cormorant races by, wings spread like an arrow flying north.

Perhaps the heron is fishing, but I know he eats small birds some-times and voles in winter, sliding the small bodies of feather and fur down his long throat. He brings twigs and grasses to his mate and she builds the nest. But he and she will take turns sitting on the nest, keeping the eggs warm until they hatch.

Pieces of Greber's design still exist: the pool at Logan Circle, the tiered bushes in the Azalea Garden, the Italian Fountain spewing silver water north of the art museum. The garden is more wild now, less cultivated. The herons like to nest in the thicket.

The fishermen have left, carrying their poles and buckets to their car. A green heron fishes in the inlet. She dips her long beak into the water, pushing at the leaf of a water lily.

# 10. Peony

ON SATURDAY WE OFTEN WALK to the hardware store to buy paint or potting soil or nails. We pass the dark stone walls of Eastern State Penitentiary constructed from 1823 to 1836 on land that was part of the north border of Thomas Penn's estate. Later there was a farm here that sold cold drinks and strawberries down the road from the waterworks.

Closed since the early 1970s, the prison is a museum now with crumbling halls, the wires of the electric chair unraveling. The design was revolutionary for prisons. Each prisoner had his own room and his own exercise run. He was given his food through a slot in the door. The designers felt that peaceful contemplation of one's sins would bring about redemption. Instead, all the inmates went crazy within a year.

The prison sits at the top of the hill where Thomas Penn's little stream flowed down into the grove of fir trees.

A guidebook to Philadelphia architecture tells me that John Haviland, the architect of the Pagoda and Labyrinthine Garden, won the competition for the design of the prison. The instructions to the architects competing for the project were: "The exterior of a solitary prison should exhibit . . . great strength and convey to the mind a cheerless blank indicative of the misery that awaits the unhappy being who enters within its walls." The interior was a variation on Sir Samuel Bentham's 1787 radial plan of seven long cell blocks, the spokes of a central rotunda. The cell blocks were long dark passageways with individual cells.

Some prisoners had gardens in the plot of land behind their cells. But unlike monks who might have cultivated their own patch of garden, they did not meet for prayers and meals. The men who lived here grew their cauliflowers and herbs and lettuces and carrots alone.

For many years after it closed the prison was a wilderness. A forest of thirty years grew up in the central rotunda. People dumped tires and trash along the perimeter.

"It's quite beautiful in there now, like a cathedral," the director of the museum told me. I was trying to get him to pick up the trash along the sidewalk in front of the iron portcullis, and he was assuring me that it was the city's responsibility, not his.

"It was in our lease when we bought the building," he said.

On warm days flocks of sparrows bend the long grasses and fruiting bushes back to eat seeds and berries along the granite walls, planted now with a garden.

Haviland purchased a piece of land near the waterworks and designed the Pagoda and Labyrinthine Garden in 1828. The pleasure garden that once surrounded the corner where our house sits now was bankrupt by 1829. His garden was in competition with three other public gardens closer to the city.

But this garden was unusual in the combination of a labyrinth and a pagoda. The original design included a Chinese temple in each corner. I think perhaps the garden was full of peonies. They're beautiful and long-lived. I know one artist who painted bushes with wide pink flowers along the perimeter. The pagoda overlooked the graveled walks and fountains of the waterworks where the landscape was still a patchwork of large estates and farms along the river. You could climb a winding stair over a hundred feet to the top and see the city to the west and country to the north. The roads were rutted and muddy in the spring.

The entrance pavilion had a "tent-like open verandah" that one critic said "evoked a Chinese spirit." The design of the garden, whimsical in contrast to Haviland's other projects, was based on William

Chamber's book on Chinese Buildings published in 1757. Chamber's book included a design for the ten-story pagoda at the Royal Botanic Gardens at Kew built for King George III. The pagoda that stood not far from my house was inspired by a trip that William Chambers took to Guangzhou when he was a boy.

I like living on the bones of a garden with a "Chinese spirit." Philadelphia has always been a place where you could cultivate your soul any way you wanted, or that was the theory.

John Bartram was disowned from the Darby Meeting because he would not state that he believed in the divinity of Jesus. He saw himself in a direct relationship with his individual God. When he finished extensive additions to his house, the stone dragged and split by hand, he carved this on the lintel below a window: "It is God Alone Almyty Lord the Holy One by Me Adord 1770 John Bartram."

His son William wrote that all things connected and entwined under a God who was the soul of all nature. Ann, John's wife, was still a member of the Darby Meeting, and even after John was disowned he continued to attend meeting for worship.

I'm not sure what I believe. We're on a corner surrounded by faith. If I walk down the street toward the river I pass the church. If I round the bend I'm on the sidewalk near the convent. And a few steps down the road I can walk up stone stairs and enter the convent of the Pink Sisters.

On my way home from the center of the city, I often stop at the corner of Green Street to walk up the steep stairs to the Chapel of Divine Love. I kneel in one of the pews and watch a woman saying the rosary. In front of us at the altar behind a golden gate is a nun. She is praying as still as a statue, the peak of her pointed habit not wavering, her pink skirts silent around her knees. Soon another sister will arrive and take up the vigil.

I'm caught up in transformations. This morning at Mass my son wiggled beside me, almost as tall as I am now. We examined the large, heavy gold candlesticks on the altar, the shiny gold hat of the baptismal. I thought about the miracle of transubstantiation, how one thing can look the same but be something else. Bread and wine transformed into Christ. I made a note to look up the definition of agnostic. Unlike William Bartram, I was certainly not convinced, yet there I was, my son leaning into my shoulder, the sun pooling in a green corner of the vaulted ceiling, Christ on the cross in a large window before me as the priest gestured his way through a sermon that made no sense.

I wonder if John Haviland felt that he needed to cleanse his spirit with a garden after he had designed a fortress for a prison.

# 11. Bamboo

MY SON LOVES THE JAPANESE TEA HOUSE reconstructed in one of the rooms of the Philadelphia Museum of Art, perched on the top of Fair Mount where a reservoir once shimmered in the heat. The tea house is delicately and strangely made and a perfect size for him. He longs to touch the bamboo fence, the slim yellow pieces held fast by black twine, or the sliding paper windows, or the little bowl with water dripping slowly from a piece of bamboo, or the woven rush mats, or the piece of rough wood that supports part of the roof, or the raked sand in the entryway, or the drainpipe made of a large stem of bamboo split in half.

I once felt the same way about a wooden structure, but I was older than my son. It was a hut in a small forest in northern Norway near a lake filled with arctic char. Men used it as a fishing shed, and people sometimes went there to pick cloudberries, those sweet-spicy salmon-colored berries of the north. I saw it only from the outside at first, a round hut made of rough wood with a sod roof. Through a square window as large as my face, I could see wooden benches built into the walls for beds and a tiny wooden table pressed under the window. It was small and perfect, sitting in a cluster of slim birch trees. I could hear the sound of a large waterfall nearby.

Graham's tea house is like that: We can't go in, silk ropes keep us away from the crawling-in door or the open sliding doors in the back. We can't partake of a ceremonial tea service there, and we can't cut the bamboo growing along the side of the walls of the artificial courtyard where it sits so still and green. Sometimes we stand and listen as the tiny stream of water drops into a rough stone bowl.

The informational cards propped near the house tell us the materials, the crawling-in door, and the overall design are to remind us of our imperfection and our oneness with nature. I'm comforted by this. My imperfection must be exquisite if it matches the beauty of this house.

Sometimes the only sound is water dripping into the stone bowl, Graham's breath, and the shuffle of feet in an adjoining gallery. But often I interrupt the silence. "Don't kick the border," I'll say to Graham, or "Don't touch the wood."

This tea house is from Tokyo, built in the style of the seventeenth century "with a certain detachment from the world."

Anne Whiston Spirn writes in her book *The Language of Landscape*: "Even a Japanese tea whisk is linked to landscape. The whisk is made from a single four-inch segment of unadorned bamboo, each filament straight and light, like a single trunk of bamboo; together they form a grove."

For me, bamboo is otherworldly. I can't believe it grows and flourishes and survives the winter. We went to our fledgling plot in the community garden not long ago and wandered around the edge where there's a new iron fence made in Montreal with iron birds and iron grasses. Near the entrance to the garden is a bed filled with a wild thicket and tall trees, an aspen as tall as the house that once stood there, a bush with frilly magenta blooms on long branches for the bees and monarchs that fly through here, a yellow spotted croton, lambs ears, and a large stand of bamboo, much taller and more established than ours.

"This is like going to the country in the city," Graham said. Flocks of goldfinches hung from the heavy heads of sunflowers, pecking at the seeds and the fruit scattered on the path.

We grow bamboo in our tiny courtyard. It's in two of several pots arranged along the back wall that we share with one of our neighbors. We dug the roots forty miles from here in Downingtown where

Scott's aunt and uncle live. His uncle pried up the roots from a stand they planted thirty years ago, hunks of hairy strands we set in big pots and covered with a light layer of earth. We've been watching the stalks grow all summer. The first batch was torn apart by a squirrel, but now another cluster of slim green shoots is sprouting up, shedding pieces of sheath like dried corn husk.

We've seen exotic bamboo in the woods here at the far northwest corner of the city in the Andorra Natural Area, a fancy title for farmland transformed into an estate and then a nursery. Now this wedge of woods is the northern tip of the Wissahickon Valley and an arm of Fairmount Park. We heard the clucking of wild turkeys and startled white-tailed deer in the green shining woods. Tulip trees two hundred years old tower over the stand of bamboo, an imported remnant from the days of the nursery, a clump of rough dark green grass near a field where deer bed down for the night. Somewhere there was the flash of the red crest of a pileated woodpecker and birds with exotic names: grasshopper sparrows, Acadian flycatchers, cerulean warblers.

Native bamboo, *Arundinaria gigantea*, or giant cane, once grew as far north as Maryland, extending canebrakes to Chesapeake bay. It grew to forty feet in large stands before European colonization and provided cover and food for turkey, deer, bear, and perhaps bison. Bamboo flowers fed animals and humans, who substituted bamboo seeds for rice or wheat.

A canebrake was a sign of fertile land. Colonists cleared it to build homes and cultivate fields. William Bartram described a Florida canebrake in the 1770s with canes "ten to twelve feet in height." In two hundred years, the vast stands have disappeared. Three birds intimately adapted to the bamboo for food and shelter had disappeared, too: the Carolina parakeet, the passenger pigeon, and Bachman's warbler, which had a bill recurved, perhaps, to peck insects from bamboo leaves. Audubon painted Backman's swamp-warbler perched on the limb of a Franklinia tree, discovered by John and William Bartram on their trip to Georgia and Florida. It was a swamp tree with large white blossoms that bloomed in the fall.

I went to the museum yesterday, thinking about bamboo. I wanted to see an exhibit of Hon'ami Koetsu, a seventeenth-century Japanese artist known for his work in calligraphy, design, and pottery. He was born in 1558 and died in 1637, straddling the turn of the century. Koetsu was one of the leaders of a renaissance of classical culture in Kyoto after a century of war. During his lifetime he was named one of the Kan'ei Sampitsu, or "Three Brushes of the Kan'ei Era." When he was older he moved to a place in the mountains called Takaga-mine. There he lived in a small village with members of his family and other artists who belonged to the Hokke, or Lotus, sect of Buddhism. They believed that happiness and universal salvation may be achieved in this world for at least two generations. I'm heartened by this.

I examined one of his tea bowls that sits in a cluster of imperfectly beautiful bowls behind glass, large, almost too large for my hands. Crackly white, this one is called Zeze Koetsu and has a nugget of gold fitted into the lip in a chip on the rim. Koetsu's tea bowls were an element at tea gatherings, a synthesis of guests, scrolls, utensils, and other objects of the tea room and the meal served. Participants kept tea diaries recording the particular elements of each gathering. As a young man Koetsu coveted and bought famous objects of tea culture. The history of his family recounts a story of Koetsu buying a tea caddy owned by the merchant Kosodeya Soze for thirty gold coins. This was considered crazy in Kyoto. To buy the caddy he sold his house for ten coins and borrowed twenty.

"In the past," he told a friend who kept a record of the conversation, "I possessed for a while some sought-after objects. Such splendid utensils were a nuisance, however 'Don't drop it!' 'Be sure not to lose it!' I finally disposed of all of them. Today, I don't own any pieces that are so desired."

After 1615 Koetsu used the name Taikyoan, or "Hut of Great Emptiness," for his tea house.

As I wander through the exhibit I read the poems translated under the illustrated poem cards:

Really how pointless
Is the cry the warbler cries
That foolish bird—
This year's not the only year
The blossoms are going to scatter.

A golden deer bends, his head almost touching his hooves. He shimmers in the autumn grasses.

Beside the woods,
grieved at distance,
through wind so dimly heard;
beneath the wall,
chanting poems of solitude,
in moonlight colors,
so cold!

The hanging scrolls are decorated with words I can't read and the swift gold images of deer and geese, grasses and bamboo. I think about the power of the swift strokes of ink, Koetsu's soul speaking in the curve of the character.

Today I watched Professor Ma, an artist in residence at my son's school, paint bamboo for a first-grade class. Famous in China, he's a master of traditional Chinese painting. His wife and translator watched with delight as he dipped first a thick brush and then a thin brush into the paint pots on the children's work table. He was sitting on a small chair, a tall thin man dressed in a dark suit. There was the bamboo stem with one stroke, the joints where the bamboo pulled itself upward, the gray-green leaf with another stroke of a smaller brush and then a panda eating a shoot of bamboo.

"What is this?" The translator asked the children. "What is the panda doing?"

"She's holding her baby," they insisted until Professor Ma was finished and they could see the panda was nibbling a bamboo shoot. At the last minute he took a fat brush thick with dark paint and with two fast strokes gave the panda a baby. He was amused as he transformed the delicate paper and finished the painting with a flourish of characters.

"He has written 'China, panda,'" the translator said.

I came home and sat in my small courtyard with a cup of tea. Ah, there's my bamboo, I thought, in its pot of soil. I felt rich in bamboo.

## 12. Thistle

NEAR US ON THE SOIL that was farmland stretching north and west from Springettsbury, the city is dissolving into chunks of mortar and brick dust. Sometimes a whole row of narrow brick houses or brownstones has vanished. Trees seed themselves in the rotting wood and brick gone back to its elements, aspens or ailanthus leaning up past the second story and then the third, right up through the roof on its way to dust. On our street thistles and pigweed grow four feet high in the cracks of sidewalks breaking up in chunks of ragged stone. Sometimes I think there's a wild garden at the end of the street.

I spoke to a woman at City Hall on the phone one day who told me she grew up near this part of the city. She remembers when block after block was still intact, and women washed their front steps and polished the stone with marble until the grain was shiny. Her husband hosed off the sidewalks on Friday when the city opened the fire hydrants to clean the streets. One woman in the neighborhood said she picks up used condoms in the street in the morning, so children won't put them in their mouths. Alleys are filled with dumped trash and nettles and saplings. Raccoons rummage in the garbage.

We live on the border of Brewerytown, the birthplace of lager beer in America. In the 1840s clipper ships transported the lager yeast brewers needed to make their beer from Germany to Philadelphia. There were, at one time, a hundred producing brewers in this part of the city. Beer from Philadelphia was shipped around the world. From Lemon Hill, the highest bluff near us, you can see the empty square buildings where the cold, thick beverage was once made.

Our neighborhood was surrounded by industry. Baldwin Locomotives had a vast factory six blocks from here where more than a thousand engines were made in over 150 different patterns in the early twentieth century. From 1918 until 1920 Baldwin Locomotives employed twenty-one thousand people. It was the biggest manufacturing company in the world.

There were even more jobs in the textile industry. A thousand companies employed thirty thousand people as pinners, operators, and other specialized jobs in the needle industry. Some of the workers or their children and grandchildren still live in the houses I can see from the lawn at Lemon Hill.

Stetson Hat Company had such a large cluster of factories and workers' houses that a bell rang in the morning to summon the workers to their tasks and the company had its own hospital. The ten-gallon hats that cowboys favored were made in Philadelphia for a hundred years and shipped to the West. Buffalo Bill Cody and his Wild West gang wore Stetsons made by hatters in the factories that were once clustered near the Delaware River. The hat was called "The Boss of the Plains."

Speculators built row after row of the houses that now, perhaps, are falling into themselves in heaps of brick and plaster and torn wallpaper.

The land Penn claimed was transformed long before the packed houses and large factories of the late 1800s. John Stilgoe, in his book *The Common Landscape of America, 1580–1845*, describes how "efficiently" the Swedish and Finnish settlers cleared the land along the Delaware river. They clear-cut the forests by *svedjebruket*, or slash and burn. This method was so destructive that "the Swedish government passed ordinances against it in the seventeenth century." Some of the violators, especially Finns, were exiled to the New World where they once again destroyed the forest.

In summer, the settlers cut deciduous trees and in winter, conifers. They let the wood dry for a year and then cut the branches off and used the largest trunks for timber. The following summer the Finnish settlers "spread the limbs and remaining trunks evenly over the ground, read incantations to the tree spirits, and fired the wood, singeing the soil. A few weeks later they sowed rye, the favorite old-country crop, and after they harvested it in the autumn, they heaped up any remaining logs and set them afire once again."

Settlers dammed and drained the marshes of Darby Creek, and their farms spread up the Schuylkill and into the rich low hills to the west. John Bartram built his stone house around the original two rooms of a Swedish settler's place. And he too drained his marshy land along the river. Interested in conservation, he rotated his crops, experimented with organic fertilizers, and grew almost twice as much hay and grain as his neighbors.

Penn instructed his steward to improve the soil at Pennsbury in this way: "I recommend to thee for the gardens & improvement of the lands, that ashes and soot are excellent for the ground, grass and corn. Soot may be got at Philadelphia, I suppose, for the fetching. I suppose it should be sewed pretty thick ... Let me desire thee to lay down as much as thou canst with English grass and plow up new Indian fields and after a crop to two they must be laid down so too; for that feeds sheep, and that feeds the ground, as well as they feed and clothe us."

John Stilgoe writes that although Penn wanted a "greene countrie towne," he was determined to build an important market town and gave up the idea of an agricultural center. He directed his agents to find a good harbor for trading ships. In three years, six hundred houses were built on the most important streets in Penn's grid. Twice a week there were large farm markets at the central square, and twice a year a fair for the colony.

Once, we drove to the southwest into land cleared in the late 1600s: miniature farms in Amish settlements stitched together like a quilt, dust blowing up in the dry fields—little rain for two weeks or so—a rolling landscape, a small cluster of buildings in the towns.

Children worked in the gardens with their parents, one strip of plowed light brown earth next to a long strip newly green. A whole family swept their dirt driveway. I admired the substantial houses and barns, a vine growing up an elaborate trellis, donkeys pulling plows, and in one field six horses as the farmers walked behind.

On Wednesday through Saturday the farmers come into Philadelphia and sell their produce and wares like the farmers did so many years ago when Penn designed his town. I've bought slim green beans in the market, an old railway terminal, and cool frilled red lettuce, firm yellow peppers, and new Yukon gold potatoes, just dug.

Here we cultivate thistle in the side bed. We're not content to watch it bloom and disperse its filmy seeds at the end of the street. I gathered the seeds in Vermont and kept them all winter, and in the spring patted them into the soil near a double sunflower, *Helianthus* × *multiflorus*. I know the thistle is invasive and destructive. I know its medicinal properties. Now the leaves are large and dark and thorny. I think about field after singed field of fallen trees, tulip, oak, birch, chestnut, and hemlock, their leaves smelling sweet that first summer on the ground, their ashes pressed into the soil the following year. Long turned under, farms gone to factories, factories gone to houses, houses gone to soil.

# 13. *Snapdragon*

PETER KALM VISITED JOHN BARTRAM in the fall of 1748 when Kalm was staying near Philadelphia. On the way from Philadelphia to Bartram's farm on the Schuylkill he passed a flower "in astonishing quantities upon all uncultivated fields, glades, hills and the like." He said the English called it "life everlasting, for its flowers, which consist chiefly of dry, shining silvery leaves . . . The English ladies are accustomed to gather great quantities of this life everlasting and to pick them with the stalks. For they put them into pots, with or without water, amongst other fine flowers which they gather in the gardens and in the fields, and place them as an ornament in the rooms." Bartram told him that the plant was also used to "bathe pained or bruised parts of the body." Did Ann, his wife, gather these flowers and decorate her rooms?

Now in the little room off the Virgin Mary's altar at St. Francis Xavier Church, I do everything wrong at first—I'm following Rose's directions and I put the oasis upside down in the deep sink and just run the water over it, can't find a stopper. I'm learning to decorate God's house.

I'm in the secret parts of the church behind the altar where I've never been before. I trod the blue and red oriental rugs and throw my vest on the back of a polished chair. I'm not robed in cream like the altar servers or wearing brocade like the priest. The cream robes hang in a row in one small wood-paneled room. In a closet off to the side, we pull out the basket with clippers and the plastic watering can. I fill the green buckets with water.

The other women arrive slowly and throw their coats off, too, and roll up their sleeves to work. When Judy comes they all shrink back a bit—she's the expert, a floral designer with a degree. She's come in from the suburbs with her station wagon full of pots of flowers and long curly willow and armfuls of greens.

We're part of a long tradition of arranging flowers for the house. When the settlers answered Penn's advertisement for a new colony they brought their traditions with them. One of the legacies was a love of flowers. Something very few of my ancestors shared. I think they were too poor in Ireland and too busy trying to grow food and raise pigs to think about the beauty of the newest discovery from Turkey or America. Some of my mother's family came from Quebec with few possessions, although my Aunt Eva and her sister Laura must have inherited their love of beautiful things from somewhere.

The designs we use in the church are the evolution of British flower arranging over several centuries. Seventeenth-century paintings show vases of flowers in public rooms that emphasize a crowning specimen, like a sunflower from the new world or an iris or tulip from Turkey. Flowers exotic to the landscape of Britain at this time and valued for their variegated petals or flower shape or color were displayed in their fluted pots.

In the eighteenth century arrangements were full and lush with the abundance of flowers that had been introduced to the wealthy landowners who coveted the new arrivals. These flowers were more natural than the arrangements of the century before as gardening styles changed in England. Some of these flowers and trees and bushes were plants John Bartram collected in Pennsylvania or the Carolinas or Florida and sent to Peter Collinson, who then sold the plants to his clients. Collinson was thrilled with one of the early plants supplied by Bartram, *Lilium superbum*, a Turk's-cap lily with brown-spotted crimson petals. He wrote to Bartram in July 1738:

Dear Frd—

I am obliged to thee for thine per Steadman, and have the pleasure
to tell thee that Most of the plants in the Last Cargo thrive finely I
never had such Luck Before that Stately Martagon thee sent found
on a bank near Schuylkill—is now Near flowering it is 5 foot ½ high
& will I believe have 15 flowers which is prodigious.

In her book *Flora Domestica*, Mary Rose Blacker writes that John
Bartram found *Magnolia grandiflora* in Bulls Bay in South Carolina
and sent it to Peter Collinson. English women liked the shiny leaves
and thick white flowers. They arranged scarlet bee balm Bartram
collected on his trip to Lake Ontario with white and blue flowers.
American plants decorated the houses of wealthy Englishmen.

Bartram was not just collecting plants, he also experimented with
the artificial hybridization of garden flowers—manipulating color
in Lychnis in 1739. He crossed red and white flowers to produce a
peach-colored bloom, according to Ann Leighton.

In the summer of 1739, Bartram wrote to his friend Colonel Byrd:
"I have made severall successful experiments of joining several species
of the same genus whereby I have obtained curious mixed colours in
flowers never known before but this requires an accurate observa-
tion & judgment to know the precise time when the femalle organs
is disposed to receive the masculine seed."

We're filling pots of flowers for Forty Hours. I'm not sure what it
is. I ask Ronnie, the leader of the group.

"You know how forty is such a big deal in the church—Jesus in
the desert for forty days and all that."

Judy tells us what to do. Don't soak the oasis until you've cut it to
fit the pot, don't press too hard, don't soak it with the holes up. We
rescue the oasis I've drenched but not soaked and use it as filler in
the vases.

"You can do the altar," she says to me, "with Ronnie."

"I'm just an apprentice," I mutter.

I concentrate on the symmetry of the flowers, first one and right and then left. I get lost in the dance of fitting the flowers into their long container. I am all flowers as I dip and bend and snip the end of a delicate snapdragon, apricot and mildly sweet, or the thick stem of a lily, the bloom still hidden.

Ronnie is talking about her son, how he loves sports.

I say, "I have an almost nine-year-old son too."

"I didn't want to ask," she says.


I fill in with frothy larkspur and the wide leaves of grapes.

A snapdragon stalk is bent in the middle.

"That's good you caught that," Judy says. "Not everyone would." Snapdragons with delicate stalks, apricot and orange, yellow mums, deep red carnations big and small, pink godetia, lacy greens like boxwood and a wide leaf like grape, goldenrod. In a way it's all bones from the curly willow on down—froth of flower in a scaffold of stem and leaf.

"Just stand back and do the squint," Judy says.

"Not bad for a rookie," Ronnie says.

Father Georges appears at my elbow and tells a story about one priest disinterred and laid to rest next to another. They were like father and son, he tells us.

It's like a dance putting the flowers into their orderly place. "Each flower has a face," Judy says.

Father Georges comes and goes and offers lunch.

"You'll never listen to the sermon from now on. You'll be looking at your flowers."

# 14. *Holly Tree*

A FEW DAYS AGO the fountains on Logan Square, one of Penn's original parks in his design for the city, were spouting ice. The naked gods and goddesses and their giant green turtles and crabs spewed a shower of glittering cold into the air. The water around the fountain was frozen too, leaves caught in solid shine. I rapped it with my fist and the surface felt stiff.

"I wonder if you could walk on this?" I asked.

"I'll try," Scott said, and he placed his left foot on the slippery shallow water, going through the ice quickly like nothing was there at all.

It's winter. The earth tilts away from the sun. Or so I hear. My husband illustrates this by swinging my son in an arc around me as I stand in the slushy street.

"The earth doesn't change," he says, "just its angle towards the sun. We're closer but farther away." The pale light of January is cold even in this latitude.

We've been sliding on a small slope below the large apartment building near Lemon Hill. When Henry Pratt lived here his greenhouse stood on the top of the hill. This time of year his lemons and citrons, exotic oranges and flowering vines would fill the glass building with sweet scent.

I push Graham from the top and Scott catches him at the bottom. He flies down the hill on a turquoise sled. By late afternoon the hill is scraped clear of snow, and leaves and pine needles have popped free from their frozen bed. At home three robins peck at the last blood-red berries of the holly tree, hop this way and that on the fence.

Today is the Epiphany. This morning at Mass I admired the painted gold branches on the altar, the light filtering down from the blue dome of the church, translucent, filled with cold. Finally the Magi have arrived and given the child his gifts, gold and frankincense and myrrh. The cold weight of the gold, the fragrance of the frankincense and myrrh, resin from trees and bushes with exotic genera: *Boswellia, Commiphora*. They've been following a bright star in the east all the way to the manger, where they know the sleeping baby is not only mortal but divine. Our deacon proclaimed the Magi astrologers.

"That's the new take on it," Scott said as we walked home from church.

In 1616 the Catholic Church banned all books that maintained that the earth moves. The planets, after all, were pushed around by angels. The earth was flat and the sun, a disc.

At the time of the first explorations of this coast by Europeans, the heavens were closer to our heads than they are now. By 1600 the dimensions of the known world had doubled, and the sky was no longer the first floor of heaven.

By the time Penn mapped the land where our house stands the universe had grown quite large. In 1609 Galileo had observed depths of space through a telescope and examined the movement of the moon and planets. He refined the telescope so he could see the night sky more clearly than anyone before him. In the cold, he wrote, the lenses became "fogged by the breath, humid or foggy air, or by the vapor itself which evaporates from the eye, especially when it is warm." In January 1610, he discovered the four moons of Jupiter: "four planets never seen from the beginning of the world right up to our day." He described his discoveries in a book called *Sidereus Nuncius* ("The Starry Messenger").

He became convinced that the earth was not the center of the universe, but rather the sun. In his defense of Copernicus he clashed with the Catholic Church in 1616 and in 1633. He was a devout Catholic. In a letter to one of his pupils he wrote:

> I believe that the intention of Holy Writ was to persuade men of the truths necessary for salvation, such as neither science nor any other means could render credible, but only the voice of the Holy Spirit. But I do not think it necessary to believe that the same God who gave us our senses, our speech, our intellect, would have put aside the use of these, to teach us instead such things as with their help we could find out for ourselves, particularly in the case of these sciences of which there is not the smallest mention in the Scriptures; and, above all, in astronomy, of which so little notice is taken that the names of none of the planets are mentioned. Surely, if the intention of the sacred scribes had been to teach the people astronomy, they would not have passed over the subject so completely.

Galileo was often sick with a recurring problem he might have picked up when he slept with friends on a hot day in a villa outside Padua. They were resting in an underground room cooled by wind from a waterfall in a nearby cave. After their two-hour nap the men complained of headaches. Soon, two of the men died and Galileo was left with rheumatic seizures that put him to bed for weeks.

When he was ill, his eldest daughter, Suor Maria Celeste, a sister in a cloistered convent near Florence, sent him marzipan shaped like fish and fresh plums, one of his biographers, Dava Sobel, tells me. Suor Maria Celeste mended and ironed his wide starched collars and his apron that he wore when he was gardening. He sent her lemons and oranges and citron he had grown in his garden. And she seeded, soaked, dried, and sweetened the fruit into candy for him.

In 1633 he was tried and sentenced by the Holy Office of the Inquisition for his book *The Dialogue of Galileo Galilei*. The cardinals on the committee felt he had committed heresy by stating once again with Copernicus that the earth moves around the sun. And although he stated during the trial that he had been mistaken, the earth does not move, he was placed under house arrest for the rest of his life. His friend Pope Urban, a poet, did not come to his defense.

Galileo watched the sky through his telescope until just before he lost his sight in 1637, confined in his villa in Arcetri near Florence. He wrote: "This universe, which I with my astonishing observations and clear demonstrations had enlarged a hundred, nay, a thousandfold beyond the limits commonly seen by wise men of all centuries past, is now for me so diminished and reduced, it has shrunk to the meager confines of my body."

At Mass the dome of the church is all the known world. I can't see the stars I have trouble naming. I don't see the earth as it moves on its axis and at the same time rotates in a precessional wobble around the sun. To me the earth may still be flat, the sun a flat disc in the sky, cut by buildings here in Philadelphia. Sometimes I'm not sure I remember the infinite nature of the sky. I read that quasars are near "the outposts of the observable universe: their redshifts indicate that their light has been traveling through space for some seventeen billion years."

I remind myself that the sky extends beyond me in what Einstein called a great eternal riddle. Scientists estimate that 4.5 billion years before the present, as Timothy Ferris writes in his book *Coming of Age in the Milky Way*, "the sun and planets congealed from a cloud of gas and dust in a spiral arm of the Milky Way galaxy."

I could lift off the ornate plaster and brick and stone of the church's roof and see far out into space if I wanted to. I'm not bound to this wobbling planet, this small street in an old city wedged between two rivers. Time extends backward and forward in all its infinite wonder. I'm not stuck here. I don't have to wait for angels to rearrange the heavens.

I think about faith and the cultivation of gardens. The improbable thought of lemons growing in a greenhouse on the hill, the cold glitter of Jupiter, Galileo's daughter condensing the fruit of her father's garden into sweet candy.

At dusk I walk with a woman to her house. She's very old and stooped, her head wrapped in a thick gray shawl. Her name, she tells me, is Marta. I'm carrying her extra packages. We've met in the grocery store.

"We've had a terrible holiday," she says and shakes her head.

"Oh, I'm sorry," I reply.

"Yes, you know the fire on Woodstock Street, that was my niece and her fiancé. They died on November 19."

"I didn't know about the fire."

"She was so young, and so kind, she had a cold and didn't go to church at five. And her fiancé had just given himself a shot, they both slept through the fire. But I think she was trying to save him, she could have gotten out the back, there was a door there. She was sick, you see, and he had diabetes, the insulin made him sleepy. They were both so young, it's a tragedy. We've had such a hard time."

We are walking through the fading light toward the northern edge of the neighborhood where it splits for Girard College, a square of stone buildings built a century and a half ago. She came to this neighborhood in 1949 from the Ukraine, the far western part, she tells me. It was Poland then.

We pass a house on the corner of a street not far from ours but a long way in the cold dusk.

"That's where the girl was raped," she says. "She jumped out the back window."

The house looks ordinary and exposed, not the kind of place someone could sneak into. The man who raped her jumped over the fence from the alley into the tiny back garden.

A few days ago in the neighborhood called Mill Creek in West Philadelphia masked gunmen broke down a door in a row house and killed seven people in what the police called "execution style." Mill Creek was buried a hundred years ago in a sewer pipe that drains the streets around the invisible banks of the brook, but the pipe is too narrow to hold all the runoff. The ground shifts and crumbles near the ghost of this tributary of the Schuylkill. In the 1880s, rows of brick houses and schools and factories were packed into the floodplain. Later some of the neighborhood was cleared for other building projects—two housing developments, playgrounds. A large community garden grows on the floodplain where the land was too wet to support houses and the porches collapsed into the soil. The house stands on the invisible banks of the creek.

"I used to read the *New York Times*," Marta says, "when I worked in the library at Drexel." We walk single file on the slippery sidewalk.

"I love English literature," she tells me as we walk north clutching plastic bags. Soon we're near her church, and the next corner is her house.

I'm blocks away from home in the early dark. I hand her the two bags I've carried and she thanks me. I run through the chill all the way home. Above me Jupiter is glittering near the first star. And all of Jupiter's Galilean moons, Ganymede, Callisto, Io, Europa, are glowing near the dark shape of its rock-filled rings.

I know the river looks frozen, but the sneaky water flows thickly over the dam past the place where Mill Creek once flowed into the Schuylkill to the Delaware and out to the ocean. I've seen where it floods the low marshy land near the coast, circles of frozen ponds on the margins of one element and another. I know fish hang in their slushy water breathing under the swirls of flat ice swept with snow. I've seen waterbirds at the throat of the river breathing near the holes where the water still flows. I hear the cold patter of the wind as it follows me south, holding on for dear life to the winter tilt of the world.

# 15. Elm

THE TIPS OF DAFFODILS and the spidery leaves of crocus and snowdrops are poking up in the bed on the side of the house.

This is a good season for pruning. I know because Locke Woodfin, an arborist, told me this on Thursday. Today is Tuesday. There are seasons in the city. I know people who don't believe this. I went to an exhibit of photographs at the museum a couple of weeks ago, and the photographer, a man who has lived for years in Philadelphia, said he didn't see the changing seasons until he lived in France. Or was it the Southwest? A traditionally spectacular place—the south of France, the American Southwest. It's important, I think, to see seasons wherever you live.

I'm attached to the notion of seasons and bound by the calendar. It's February, the edge of spring here, although the calendar tells me I have almost another month until it's official. The cardinal singing his spring song on the top of a lanky bare tree in the azalea garden knows that the winter has turned a corner. The rowers in their long shiny boats pulling toward the mouth of the Schuylkill know this too; they've been on the water for about a week now.

When Locke Woodfin came to look at our three elm trees he told me that they were Siberian elms. Finally I have a specific name for them.

The elms leafed out give us a dappled street. A light breeze lifts their delicate leaves and fluffs them down again. I love their mossy green limbs, their tiny round seeds that carry their own packet of potting soil so they sprout with the least moisture on the street in the spring. Our familiar pigeons peck at the transparent samaras the size of a nickel, scattered on the black pavement like confetti.

I like the elms' slow leafing out, so slow I fear for their health all through spring. Their leaves in the summer are thick and serrated.

In the fall they turn a deep gold and shine this way and that in the warm October sun. In rain they're shimmery trees, resilient and old. They bend their branches and touch the roof or the telephone line in the front of the house or the wooden edge of the deck.

I watched a yellow-bellied sapsucker drill several large holes in the elm in front of the house a few days ago. She was tapping the trees for sap. She sipped the sweet liquid as it collected on the rim of each hole she had drilled.

Sometimes great limbs fall off onto the street. And that's what Scott is afraid of, a limb crashing onto someone's car or worse yet, someone's head.


"We're lucky to have these trees in our neighborhood," Locke Woodfin said. He lives around the corner on Woodstock Street.

"My neighbors don't like the elms," I told him. "Mary Robinson wants the city to cut hers down."

"They won't do it," he said. "Tell her you'll pull up the sidewalk and build a garden box around it like this one," he said.

"Are you kidding," Scott said when I told him later. "With everything else we have to do?"

Fairmont Park Commission owns the trees, but we're responsible for pruning. In Penn's time Lord Baltimore had his men mark the old trees south of here with his crest just to make sure William Penn knew where his land ended and Lord Baltimore's began.

In September 1683 Penn's agent in Pennsylvania wrote to him in England:

Most Excellent Sir

There is a report that the Lord Baltimore is arrived at the head of the (Chesapeake) Bay & that he has run a line piercing into part of your lands, having particularly surveyed John Darby's plantation, and cut his (coat of) arms on several remarkable trees.

Our trees are healthy, Locke told me.

"Look at all the good bud development. They just sap out like that from old wounds."

He gave me three estimates for pruning, all too expensive for us. We'll probably go with the cheapest, prune the branches over the house and take off some weight on the branch that extends onto the deck.

"I'd cut that one right off there," he said and pointed to a crook in the limb of the tree.

"Oh no I've got to keep that one," I said. "We like that one." We stood in the center of the street bending back to see sky and limb and branch.

"They're not as old as they look," he said. "Maybe fifty years."

He told me the tree down the street is a silver maple.

"They thought they were good street trees when they put them in," he said, "but we don't plant them anymore."

William Penn bought the land where I live from the Lenni-Lenape, and after his purchase the Lenape called it Penn's Woods. Their territory stretched from Maryland to New York and from the Atlantic to the western edge of the Delaware River watershed. By 1680 the Lenape had been in contact with Europeans for at least eighty years. Penn wanted to deal peacefully with his neighbors. And although the King of England had given him a large chunk of forest and river in payment of a debt to Penn's father, Penn wanted to purchase the land from the people who lived here.

In the first letter he sent to Lenape representatives through his agent in the colonies, he wrote: "Now this great God has been pleased to make me concerned in your parts of the world, and the King of the country where I live has given unto me a great province therein, but I desire to enjoy it with your love and consent, that we may always live together as neighbors & friends, else what would the great God say to us, who has made us not to devour and destroy one another, but live soberly and kindly together in the world." In 1682 he signed the famous treaty at Shackamaxon on the Delaware River under a huge tree that stood until the early 1800s.

The Lenape sold a large tract of land that included the site of Philadelphia for belts of wampum, blankets, stroudwater (blue and red cloth), kettles, guns, coats, stockings, cups, hoes, axes, powder, lead, knives, small glasses, 20 pairs of shoes, 40 copper tobacco boxes, tobacco tongs, a small barrel of pipes, 40 pairs of scissors, 40 combs, awls, pistols, 2 handfuls of fishhooks, one handful of needles, duck shot, 10 bundles of small beads, 20 glass bottles, 5 small saws, tobacco, rum, cider, beer, and other European items that they had been using for some years.

This same tract of land had been sold in 1675 to a representative of the governor of New York. There were very few people living in the wedge of land between the Delaware and the Schuylkill rivers at this time. Penn's companions in his Holy Experiment built their houses in the footsteps of an abandoned town.

By the time Philadelphia first took shape along the marshy banks of the Delaware and then spread in a neat grid all the way to the Schuylkill, the land was less than an Indian ghost town. Only the oldest Lenape could remember the significance of a certain tree (a place where they had fastened captives for the night) or a narrow trail on a ridge bordered with huckleberries, the site of a conjurer's hut. Penn's Woods were washed clean of a spiritual connection to the Lenape, Iroquois, or Shawnee neighbors who lived and hunted on the edge of this land. Settlers constructed a new history on the territory they called their own.

I've wandered in Penn's woods along the Wissahickon several times since my first long walk there in the fall. I've hiked along a narrow path above the creek on shiny mud and stood under the tulip trees still bare of leaves now reaching up into the clear sky all this winter. I've seen the swirling waters flowing over rocks and wandered near a little bridge cut in the cliff above the water. I walked up to a house that was once part of the underground railroad and stood silently watching horses and ponies pawing the earth in a corral. I've thought about the spine of woods traveling from the north to the south of the city, an extensive garden of trees. I've thought about the muskrats paddling in their shallow waters at the mouth of the Wissahickon and the muskrats slipping into Darby Creek near the mouth of the Schuylkill. Smooth bodies traversing their geography of water. I've tried to see the city as a whole carved out of meadow and woods and water.

Now as I write the squirrel pulls an elm branch into her mouth and bites off the sweet red buds. Soon the little leaves, slender and light green, serrated at the edge, will pop. Part of the unfurling going on all over Penn's Woods in these almost-spring days.

# 16. Skunk Cabbage

I WAS THINKING ABOUT A FOX YESTERDAY as we drove home. We had been to a place where whistling swans spend a few weeks on their way to the Arctic. They fatten up for the journey north after their weeks flying as far as Pennsylvania from the south. We wandered along a trail in the woods through scotch pine and beech and along a wooden path through a swamp, dry now after weeks of drought. The tips of skunk cabbage were poking up in the moss, their thick veined skins arched like a large thumb.

The swans were flying in large flocks of a hundred or more, but we watched a few gathered near the road. They clucked like chickens, their soft, bubbly voices calling to each other across the startling blue pond.

I felt like I was seeing the world with new eyes—just like those early explorers, the sky heavy with birds.

I imagined the fox following us home from the game lands near Lancaster all the way across farmland and woods to the outskirts of the city. I thought about what she would do once she got past Gladwyne. I saw her running along the river near the railroad tracks and then, when she could, running up the hill to the west side of Fairmount Park where she could build a den and live in the remnants of Penn's woods. There's a gray fox who lives near Bartram's garden. Her territory is a small acreage of marsh and field and garden along the river.

I suppose I was thinking about the fox because I felt more bound to the earth than the swan. I thought maybe I was a little like the fox. I felt nostalgic for woods right outside my door. I felt the hardness of the pavement once I stepped from the car into the parking lot and walked across the street and along the sidewalk and into my house. I was surrounded by a hard landscape that I try to ignore. I'd been walking for a couple of hours on pine duff and boards and leaves.

I'm not migratory. I have nested here in the middle of a very large city near the banks of a wide shallow river that sometimes smells like the ocean. A river that at its mouth mixes with the salt of the sea come all the way up from the mouth of the Delaware. Sometimes I see birds here that you wouldn't expect in Philadelphia at all. Last week I found a dead woodcock by the large windows of the university where I teach.

I knew the bird was some kind of wading bird—very large, like a grouse with a long narrow beak and feathers dipped and marked in chocolate and long yellow feet. I wanted to pick the woodcock up but I didn't. I stooped for a long time over the body of the bird, wondering why it had flown into the windows on a warm late February day.

When I got home I was surprised to read that the bird may have been blown by the winds or disoriented, migrating north early and alone. Woodcocks live in low thickets in damp places and set up a singing ground in the spring.

In the fall I found an owl dead on the edge of the road near the Chapel of Divine Love a block away from our house. He was perfectly made with tufts of creamy brown feathers on his legs like furry socks and fierce claws and a halo of stippled feathers above his eyes. He was not much bigger than my husband's hand—a saw-whet owl. "A very tame little owl," Peterson's field guides states, who sings "too, too, too, too" a hundred times a minute. He might have been wintering here, his summer range north and east of Philadelphia. The next day, the body had vanished.

Animals arrive in improbable places in the city, claiming the place as their own wild garden. Someone, perhaps a game commission officer, shot a deer in my friend Ann's backyard last spring. She told me she came home from doing some errands and there were eleven policemen at the house. By the time she had arrived all the drama was finished. The deer was dead. There was only the body of the deer and his blood and hair on the fence around their yard, a small yard connected to other small yards in a square behind her house.

He was a young deer, she told me, his horns were just starting to sprout. Neighbors wondered if he had come up from Tinicum or crossed over from the Cobbs Creek watershed.

"Funny to see a deer right in your backyard in Philadelphia," she said as we waited to hear our children read their stories to us in an event called "Meet the Authors."

"Yes," I said.

I was feeling confused about where I was. Deer in the backyards. Of course, I thought to myself, they had to shoot the deer. It seemed like the only conclusion to a story that had eleven policemen and a city neighborhood and blood and hair on an iron fence. I was amazed at how cold I felt about the whole thing.

"The policemen," I said, "were probably relieved it wasn't a body."

When I tried to think about the deer I couldn't feel anything. I had spoken to Jerry Czech, wildlife conservation officer for Philadelphia County, a couple of weeks before. I asked him what a conservation officer does in Philadelphia.

"Oh," he said, "I mostly track down illegal hunters, take samples from dead deer and send it to Harrisburg for analysis, contents of the stomachs, size of the jaw, fetuses." He told me bow and arrow hunters can take 150 deer legally in Philadelphia. Recently, Anne Raver reported in the *New York Times* that "in the last four years, sharpshooters have culled 1,200 deer from two parks—Wissahickon in the west and Pennypack in the northeast." Coyotes in the city kill deer, too.

In the Wissahickon volunteers have erected deer fences to protect native plants. When I walked in the northernmost section of the park I saw several of their small slim bodies, white tails flipped up, as they ran in the dark green woods. I figured a deer who blundered into the tight knot of houses and businesses where Ann lives wouldn't have much of a chance of coming out of the adventure alive.

Peter Kalm in his *Travels* sketches the richness of the wildlife in Philadelphia in the 1750s when Thomas Penn's Springettsbury was clipped and ordered and John Bartram was developing his American garden. Bartram told him there were many bears in the hills and teased him with stories about air pressure that toppled trees and bears that killed cows by biting a hole in their sides and blowing air into them. Kalm described woodchucks, raccoons, white-tailed deer, gray foxes, and gray squirrels in the hundreds that covered fields and destroyed crops of corn. He was charmed by red squirrels and kept some in cages.

By the end of the nineteenth century the wolf, black bear, mountain lion, bobcat, beaver, white-tailed deer, and elk had disappeared from the Philadelphia area. It was still wild here when Kalm was discussing plants with John Bartram.

I think the city is strangely rich in wildlife now. Deer reappeared early in the twentieth century, along with wild turkeys and coyotes, though no one knows how many. I've seen a dead woodchuck on the lawn at the art museum. Raccoons live in the alleys, and my neighbor caught a baby opossum that was eating her impatiens. Some animal is nibbling my striped Japanese forest grass in the side garden and the sharp tips of daylily leaves. We have small black rats. The red fox, introduced for fox hunting in the mid-eighteenth century, lives in all parts of Fairmount Park. The gray fox and chipmunk live in the woods, and the star-nosed mole likes shallow marshy places. Beavers sometimes wander into the city. Cottontail, and short-tailed shrew, meadow vole, house mouse, white-footed mouse, Eastern mole, and muskrat are also listed in the "Fairmount Park Natural Lands Restoration Master Plan."

The city acts as a wildlife sanctuary for breeding birds. Ornithologists consider Philadelphia important for songbirds including thrushes, vireos, flycatchers, wood warblers, tanagers, and orioles. Owls, hawks, swallows, ducks, and woodpeckers have also been recorded in the park. The great horned owl and the pileated woodpecker live in the thickest forests.

Pieces of the park are the fragile outlines of a large wild garden.

The sky cleared today from snow and rain and I drove to the Wissahickon with a friend. We walked slowly along the creek. No one else was in the woods. The drive was newly graveled, and the trees bore no sign of spring buds just a little uphill from the magnolia trees about to burst near the river. This morning I saw one yellow bloom unfurling in the snow. The tulip trees and beech trees are taller than any trees I know of on the East Coast. Today as I bent my head back to look at the interstices of branch and sky I felt I was looking at an enormous height. The only sound was the water running coldly over stones and logs and the shallow sandy rills of the creek bed. I knew there were deer nipping the tiny leaves of spring flowers poking up along the hillsides. I liked being suspended between winter and spring, the confluence of green-ribbed leaf and snow.

# Kingsessing

## THE FINEST
## RELISHED FRUITE

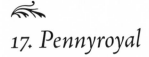

# 17. *Pennyroyal*

ANN BARTRAM, THE WIFE OF JOHN BARTRAM, the King's botanist, and the mother of William Bartram, famous for his book of travels to the wilds of Georgia and Florida, had a garden southwest of our house, five miles down the Schuylkill. She lived on the river at the bend called Kingsessing in the second half of the eighteenth century. Her kitchen garden was ordered and fruitful, growing not far from the door of her house. This time of year she would be harvesting spinach and peas, the first leaves of lettuce, and parsley.

I have a hard time imagining her life 250 years ago on the bank of the river. She was twenty-six when she married Bartram in December 1729. His first wife had died, and one of his young sons died a year after her death. Ann's first child was born when she was twenty-six, her last when she was forty-five. They moved to their farm with John's young son Isaac.

When her husband was away from his large farm collecting plants for his gardens and for subscribers in Britain and Europe on long journeys north to the Great Lakes or south to Florida, she took care of his correspondence and shipped plants and seeds to Thomas Jefferson or Peter Collinson in England or gardeners in Charleston, South Carolina.

Martha Logan, a friend of John Bartram and author of one of the first American gardening calendars written for South Carolina, "Directions for Managing a Kitchen Garden every month of the year Done by a Lady," sent Ann a letter in 1761 while John was hunting plants:

Madam

I received your favour by Captain North, and am much obliged for taking the trouble of answering mine, in Mr. Bartram's absence. I hope he is, by this, returned to his family, and well. Pray, give my respects to him, and tell him I should be very glad he would tell Mr. Ratlive what the *Andromeda*, on the road he mentioned to me, is,— and I will most certainly get it, and send at a proper season. But I cannot find it out from Doctor Garden.

Mr. Ratlive is my neighbour, and will inform me better than any letter can.

I herewith send some roots of the Indian or Worm Pink, as the seeds were all fallen, before I had yours about them.

In the same tub, are some slips of Mrs. Bee's little flower, lest the seeds should fail. The berries on the trees are not yet ripe enough; but if I live, your spouse may certainly expect them, with the other things. I am with great truth, your well-wisher and friend,

Martha Logan

Ann Bartram's reply has vanished.

Shipments to England had to survive the long journey by boat. Seeds were wrapped in paper, nuts packed in dry sand, trees in barrels, and roots wrapped in moss, according to Ann Leighton in her book on eighteenth-century gardens. Bartram's seeds were sometimes shipped loose in a box with dividers or layered with moss or straw. The tiny or valuable seeds were sent in paper.

In January 1734, Peter Collinson wrote to John Bartram thanking him for "thy Two Choice Cargos of plants." This was one of the first letters of a thirty-four-year correspondence between the two men. Captain Wright had a "Little Case of plants" under his bed "& saw not the Light," Collinson writes, "till I sent for it." The skunk weed blossomed in the heat of the ship. "The Laurell & Shrub Honeysuckle are plants I much Value," he noted.

The outline of John Bartram's botanic garden still survives in a slope down to the river, the original line of trees marching to the bank of the wide shallow tidal rush. A drawing of the garden that William Bartram made in 1758 and his father sent to Collinson shows the garden and the house from the river. There's a path from the house to the riverbank and steps down to the water. William has drawn his father pausing in the garden, leaning on a staff. On the opposite bank someone is fishing, and a boat is tethered near a marshy area to the right of the path to the river.

There's a pond in the middle of the drawing and three lines of trees to the left. Near the house in a neat fence is a "new flower garden" under the windows of a structure marked "my study." The common flower garden is directly in front of the house, to its right is the upper kitchen garden, and below that, covering the large space above the pond, is the lower kitchen garden. Beyond these enclosed gardens pictured in the drawing were fields where crops were grown, a barn, a dairy, a cider mill, and an orchard. Smoke curls in puffs above the two chimneys on the house.

In 1760 John Bartram built a greenhouse. Ann would have tended those plants when he was traveling. Bartram grew a sponge tree sent by Martha Logan, pineapple, Persian cyclamen, Italian strawberry, gardenia, oleander, geraniums, and a pomegranate.

I went to the garden a few days ago. I found fox scat curled in one of the beds. Birds were experimenting with their songs in the large trees by the water.

I saw the courtyard where Ann Bartram saved a small striped snake from the mouth of a larger snake and the place where she cooked her meals in the house her husband designed and built on the foundation of an old Swedish homestead. I walked through the small rooms where her nine children slept and where her son William wrote his famous book about his travels. I ran my hand on the banister of the narrow steps that ascended to the second floor. I admired the stone of the dairy where she milked her cows, the order of the garden where she planted herbs, and the path where she walked to the river's edge to press cider in a stone carved out near the water for that purpose. I smelled the air of the tiny rooms where she lived, and I felt the cold stone of the pillars ornately twining on the front of the porch. I imagined her reading letters from Peter Collinson when her husband John was collecting new plants. Once he was away for five weeks searching in Maryland and Virginia and traveled, he calculated, eleven hundred miles.

I could hear her moving the plants in their pots to near the house. I could see her hands as she wrapped the plants in moss for the journey to England, as she sorted the seeds and then changed her youngest son's diaper.

I'd been reading her husband's letters, his record of the journey to New York and the council place of the League of the Iroquois, Onondaga. I could hear her son in his letters to his mother and father, in his beautiful *Travels*, and his cryptic, meticulous garden diary.

But she has left no record of her voice. The evidence is that she was strong, in good health much of the time, industrious, and thoughtful. Or at least that's what I imagine. She was accomplished with healing herbs, as were her husband and son William.

John made a list of some of the medicinal plants that the Bartrams grew in their garden: stargrass, which "easeth the Pains of the stomach," and wild sarsaparilla for cleansing the blood; spikenard, or "Wild liquorice" to cure fresh wounds; butterfly root and devil's bit; horse balm for "Womens After—pains"; great lobelia, bloodroot, and lizard's tail; and culver's root, used for a "powerful Vomit."

She had large kitchen gardens near her house, kept cows, and may have had a small business selling butter and milk. Once a friend of John Bartram's, Sir John St. Clair, who had an estate in New Jersey, sent her a cow. His letter of November 1761 instructs: "If you will send any Body to this place to bring a cow for Mrs. Bartram she will oblige me in accepting her. She is of the famous Rhode Island breed and will calve at Christmas; they are of a very large Size, if her Calf is not a Bull I shall rear one of mine for you that you may preserve that valuable breed which cost me a great deal of trouble to get."

Each day was a complicated symphony of chores: carrying wood for the fire, cooking and spinning perhaps, sweeping the polished floors, feeding and washing and putting her children to bed. Ann Bartram's occupations as a wife and mother in the 1700s were almost exactly the same as the women who lived 150 years before her in the early settlements in New England and Virginia.

In the kitchen she probably used the wooden bowls that her mother used, as china cups and plates were rare. She may have been given a teacup and saucer by Deborah Franklin, Benjamin Franklin's wife. The chipped cup and saucer are in her house still, kept by family members all these years. Her pots were iron or wooden or copper, and some stood on tripods near the fire. She worked with wooden utensils and used long iron poles and chains to adjust the heat in the large fireplace. Her kitchen floor would have been scrubbed clean with soap, water, and a little sand each day, polished with the grains, and the walls of the kitchen and the other rooms in the house were whitewashed each year.

The kitchen was the place where meals were cooked, clothes sewn, fruit sorted, seeds put up in packets, and herbs dried. Children studied their lessons here, and perhaps John wrote his letters to Peter Collinson. In the winter it was the warmest room in the house, and it was where Ann probably spent much of her time. In many early settlements the kitchen *was* the house—rooms were added only several years later, when the settlers had time and money.

Ann Bartram had to maneuver in the kitchen in long skirts, with the fire always glowing on the hearth; she had to kindle the fire and then tend the coals, swinging heavy pots off lug-pole hangers. The only way to test the heat of the oven at the side of the huge fireplace was to thrust your hand into the heat. In the fall, besides pressing juice from her harvest of apples for cider, she would be drying racks of slices in the sun or putting up crocks of apple butter and sauces.

The Bartrams may have grown several kinds of apples on the farm. Frances Phipps in her book *Colonial Kitchens* mentions one seventeenth-century list of apples for "kitchen use" which includes codling, summer marigold, summer red pearmain, Holland pippin, Kentish pippin, Loan's pearmain, *pomme violette*, Spencer's pippin, Stone pippin, oakenpin, monstrous reinette, French reinette, French pippin, royal russet, and winter pearmain. There were also several apples good for dessert and six especially for cider. How can I understand a woman who may have grown several types of apples for specific culinary purposes in an orchard near her house?

I'm overwhelmed by the details of John Bartram's life, letters and journals he left and descendants preserved, and the lists and drawings of William Bartram, his notations in his daybooks, his book of travels. What I don't know about Ann Bartram sends me shuffling to old books and letters written at the time when she lived. I have no idea what she was like. What kind of apple she liked for pies or sauce. Which apple smelled the sweetest as she pulled it with a snap from the branch. She worried about her son William when he tried to start a plantation in Florida and later when he wandered for four years in the wild Southeast and they hardly ever heard from him. She doctored her family with herbs she grew, nursed her husband John after he was a kicked by a horse and cracked his ribs. Once he fell out of a tree and broke his leg while collecting pine cones for an English gardener.

We know her husband was "Botanist to His Majesty for the Floridas" and was respected as one of the leading scientists of the time. He was clever and curious. Her son William, an artist, was also a botanist and explorer. Ann's skills extended to the perimeter of her husband's land. She lived in Kingsessing on the bones of an old Swedish farm, cultivated her garden, fed her large extended family, and helped her husband in his occupations. Only one or two of her letters have survived.

I held a letter in my hands yesterday written by John Bartram in September 1761 to his son William who was trying to become a merchant in the Carolinas, one of the first of a succession of failed business ventures. He was twenty-two and had not liked anything yet that he had tried his hand at, except for drawing and exploring with his father. At the very bottom of the letter Ann Bartram had written a few words, one of the few examples of her writing that has survived. My hand was close to her hand as I read the words she wrote:

Dear bill I joyn with thy father in the good counsel hee give thee
wishing thee health and prosperity in all thy undertaking desiring
to hear from thee at all opertunitys and if I have anny in thy fathers
absence I shall write to thee
from thy loving mother
Ann Bartram

I looked at the letter for a long time. I was sitting at a library table in the New York Historical Society. I wondered who sold the letters and who bought them and how they traveled here. The letter was yellowed, the ink faded to brown. Pieces of the paper were missing on the edges, and it had been folded and refolded and sealed with red sealing wax when it was first sent from Philadelphia to William Bartram Marchant in Cape Fear. When William came back to Philadelphia and his father's house he was in debt. He took the letter home with him and kept it.

His mother's writing is less steady than her husband's. Maybe she was holding a grandchild on her hip as she wrote, maybe she was in a hurry, something cooking to check on the hearth, maybe her youngest child, Benjamin, who was eleven, was calling her outside. It was September and very warm, perhaps, as Septembers are here. She wrote in haste, her letters not even, the script going up and down across the page, the word "father" inserted above the first line. Perhaps she said, I'll just scribble something to Bill and picked up the pen her husband was using, dipped it quickly into the ink and wrote . . .

When I lived in Oxford, England, for a year, I was younger than William was when he lived in the Carolinas. My father was worried about me, too. He never wrote letters. I hardly remember him writing at all, but he would scribble something to me on the back of those thin airmail letters my mother wrote. I've kept them in a box somewhere, one of the few batches of letters I've stored away. One day I shredded most of the others. Now my father is gone, too, like the Bartrams dead so many years before. And his small gestures like Ann's note to her dear bill on the bottom of her husband's letter continue to reassure me.

I'm planting the seeds of my herbs. In a couple of months or so, I can harvest the bitter lemon thyme and clean lavender, the tiny blooms of bright blue borage pulled into a point, the thick garlic chives and frilly feverfew, the narrow blue sage and the pointed leaves of the rosemary tree, a small slip of tarragon.

# 18. *Marsh Grass*

I'M SHOVELING UP COAL DUST, pieces of horsehair plaster, spiky sections of brittle lath, and puckered wallpaper in a house not far from Bartram's garden. We're in the flats across the river. On old maps the area is designated as marsh, part of the vast soggy plain that once bordered the mouth of the Schuylkill. John Bartram drained some of this marsh for his fields. Rich sloping land along the river. The neighborhood borders Sunoco's round oil tanks on the shore. From Bartram's garden you can see across the river to the edge of this grid of streets, row after row of two-story houses built at the turn of the century, clustered around their dark-stoned churches and large square schools.

For a long time no one built anything here. The man I'm working with, Joe, grew up in the neighborhood a few streets away.

"In Colonial times," he tells me, "they wouldn't build here, too wet. It's all fill."

The blocks of red brick buildings and empty factories with jagged broken windows, the empty stores and treeless streets are not what William Penn had in mind when he described his plans for the city. He was given a new land by the King of England to settle a debt to his father and could afford to be visionary about city planning. He owned a whole chunk of land with good forests and fertile fields and two lovely rivers. He chose a separate spot on the Delaware for his manor house, but the city was designed to fit between the Delaware and the Schuylkill and endowed with five public squares "for the comfort and recreation of all forever."

He wrote, "Let every house be placed, if the person pleases, in the middle of its plat as to the breadth way of it, that so there be ground on each side for gardens, or orchards, or fields, that it may be a greene countrie towne which will never be burnt and will always be wholesome."

By the late eighteenth century the city was still green. People grew herbs and fruits and vegetables in their backyards and in the open spaces on the edges of the rows of houses. Factories had eliminated most of those gardens by the end of the nineteenth century, when Philadelphia was the most industrialized city in the country.

I learn from Patricia Hynes in her book *A Patch of Eden* that "a tiny backyard held the privy and coal bin, but gardens that had served to compost human and animal waste, to provide fresh food, and to drain rain and waste water from habitats, were sacrificed to land-intensive industrialization."

Penn was interested in making money, but he also saw the value in preserving the natural wealth of his colony. Ann Leighton, in her book on eighteenth-century gardens, tells me he urged that "in clearing the ground, care be taken to leave one acre of trees for every five cleared, especially to preserve oak and mulberries for silk and shipping."

As early as 1700 developers had subdivided house lots and constructed skinny alleys down the middle of blocks. There were two thousand brick houses by this time.

Joe works for a group called Community Home Repair, an organization that works to help neighbors fix their houses at no or low cost. I'm the supervisor of several ninth graders from Scott's school. I'm being paid to accompany them, though I feel I would rather volunteer.

"It must be something legal," Scott said when I objected.

We're a funny group. I wore a long raincoat over my jeans and sweater and I've bunched it in a wad at the base of the stairs. The boys and girls, children, really, fifteen or fourteen, are in T-shirts and dust masks. Muhammad, who is very tall, has been given the task of pulling wet ceiling tiles down from the first-floor room.

The house is small: a living room and kitchen on the first floor, and three tiny bedrooms on the second and a bathroom that we can't use. The water's turned off. It's Brenda Jackson's house.

When we arrived she was standing in the living room waiting for us. There are no lights in the house. It's a dark day. I can't breathe when we walk into the room—but I know it's because I can't see. I wonder how we'll work here. We pull the curtain aside on the one front window and light creeps into the room. On the second floor it's lighter and I prop a few windows open.

Brenda's had water damage in the house. She bought it twenty years ago with her husband but separated from him a couple of years ago. She has two daughters, six and eight, she tells me, and soon they'll move back into the house. They've been gone from the house for two years.

"It was real nice," she says.

"It will be again soon," I say cheerfully. But I've never seen a house in such bad shape.

Her husband has died and she's repairing the house with the help of Community Home Repair and the groups of students and teachers and two men who work full-time for the organization, which is affiliated with a church in the suburbs.

The streets in this neighborhood have no trees, no pots of flowers on the stoops, nothing growing on street after street. We've walked through the rain to get here, winding our way from the storefront where we met Joe to Brenda's house several blocks away. The students hunched their shoulders and shuffled along the sidewalk.

Susan Strasser, an expert on trash, writes that before the twentieth century "in cities ragmen worked the street, usually buying bones, paper, old iron, and bottles as well as rags . . . 'Swill children' went from house to house in American cities collecting kitchen refuse to sell for fertilizer or hog food. Others foraged for shreds of canvas or bits of metal on the docks, for coal on the railroad tracks, and for bottles and food on the streets and in the alleys."

I looked at a book a few days ago that had pictures taken by reformers bent on cleaning up the city in the first decade of this century, just when these houses were being mortared into position, brick by brick. Barrels of refuse lined the street. In front of a family who had posed for the photographer, there were piles of junk, slices of wooden wheels, shattered brooms, and matted rags. The trash now is less picturesque: colored candy wrappers, newspapers, smashed cigarette boxes, plastic bags, airborne or plastered to the sidewalks or in the rain gutters.

Philadelphia was not as green then. A few years later developers cut a swath through some of the crowded row houses northwest of here and built a parkway modeled on the Champs Elysees. Suddenly there was a corridor of parkland leading north.

When I walk on the dirt path along the Parkway I stumble over bricks popping up in the dirt, the last pieces of houses pulled down for the new landscape.

Brandon is holding the big black plastic bag so I can dump the debris into the bottom. He's just pulled down most of the ceiling and now is working on the walls. He takes a crowbar and pulls hard so the lath splinters and pulls away from the studs. Coal dust covers everything. Our faces are black and smudged with almost a hundred years of it in the walls.

In the other bedroom the students are yelling. Tarik has found a large cockroach half the size of my hand and refuses to pick up the pile of plaster rubble at his feet because the cockroach is in the middle.

"It's dead," I say and shovel it into the bag.

I've never seen anything like this bug, light brown, like the underside of a horseshoe crab and its chitinous gills that crack easily. I used to watch my brother and his friends split crabs in two on the metal spikes of a bridge in the shallows of the ocean creek where we sometimes spent our summers. Why didn't I stop them, I wonder.

Joe supervises the work in the front bedroom. He has Sarah and Ashley screw plywood on top of the damaged wooden floors so Brenda can have carpet laid. The students' teacher asked me to have Sarah and Ashley go with Dave, the head of Community Home Repair, but they've ended up with Joe. Last time they volunteered Joe treated them like delicate girls, something they didn't like. This time he seems fine. He shows them what to do and they do it. They move along the floor on their hands and knees pressing the plywood into the old floor, securing it along the edges. Soon they've almost finished the whole room.

"I grew up here, a couple of streets away," Joe tells me. "I just bought a house near here. A lot of work left though, and I can only do it after work here. I just finished ripping out the kitchen."

His right arm is missing below the elbow and he uses his arm like a hand, holding a piece of twine down while he cinches in the bag I've just finished loading.

"When I was two years old, I got hit by a bus, just around the corner from here, cut my arm off."

"I'm sorry," I say.

"It's okay," he shrugs, "it's been like this a long time." His plaid shirt is rolled up tightly above the end of his arm.

"I went to school here, too," he says as we stand in the street, breathing air not filled with plaster dust.

"I'm gonna die, I can't breathe," Lee says as he staggers out of the screen door. He whips off his dust mask. His mouth is ringed in black.

Back inside Yufan and Rajiv have found a nest in the tiny back bedroom.

"Look at this," they yell, and Brenda, back from a meeting, examines the piles of straw on the floor, looks up at the pieces of twine and grass poking from the rafters.

"Well, look at that," she says. "I never knew we had that there."

"It won't kill the babies, will it?" Lee asks.

"Oh no," I say, "I think it's an old nest." But all the time I'm thinking about mice and hantavirus.

"It's a pigeon nest probably," Joe tells me later. "They're smart birds. They probably got in when there was a hole in the roof. They've fixed it now. Yes, very smart birds, in the winter they huddle close to the house."

I've watched two pigeons who visit our sidewalk, a small slate blue male and his companion, a large white female, one of her claws bent under into a pink fist, as she hops from crumb to crumb. I'm fond of the pigeons, their sturdy bodies, their little feet. One morning I read an article in the *New York Times* that proclaimed pigeons are monogamous and can help find people lost at sea.

Even "ten day old pigeons have enough feathers to keep themselves warm in any weather." The birds adjust the angle of their feathers, increasing or decreasing the layers. On a cold day they push their feathers out like a down parka; on a warm day their feathers are "compressed," held close to the body. "They raise their young on 'crop milk,' a mix of regurgitated food and salivary enzymes," a milkshake for baby pigeons. Their back feathers break away in the mouth of a hungry dog, leaving a fluff of feathers instead of a plump pigeon. Skilled at escaping and at finding their way home, they can hear sounds that humans can't but have only thirty-seven taste buds compared to our nine thousand.

City pigeons are food for peregrine falcons. Not long ago Graham and I watched a young peregrine sitting on a lamppost. She was twice the size of a pigeon, puffed up in the cold, her feathers brown and white, the sharp profile of her curved beak stark against the bright blue sky. We thought she was hunting the pigeons pecking at the dirt, their feathers fluffed out in the chilly wind.

Suddenly she was off, swooping toward the scuffed dirt and then up to a tall oak where she scattered a dark bunch of starlings from their perch. Her dive looked like a practice run.

My guide book tells me that our bird was probably a juvenile, more brown than her parents. Once called the duck hawk, she can dive at two hundred miles per hour toward her prey.

This bird's parents may have mated for life. They performed courtship dives and circled each other, and the male presented a pigeon, perhaps, to the female.

Brenda has borrowed a broom from a neighbor, and I think about the pigeons as I sweep and shovel debris into a plastic bag. I wonder if there were pigeons here in the marsh. I wonder what it was like, the marsh filling with water at high tide and then emptying out at low, the cycle that refreshed itself again and again.

When we take a break, the students use the broom as a baton.

"You'll break it," I warn them.

And they do.

# 19. Oranges

WHEN WILLIAM BARTRAM RETURNED from his years of travel in the wild parts of Florida and Georgia all the way to the banks of the Mississippi he rode his horse home.

He was alone and traveled north in the winter on the sandy hard beaches of the Carolinas, a solitary man on a horse trotting across the yellow sands on the edge of the Atlantic. He had been in the vast wild garden of Florida for several years. He came home quietly, first stopping to visit his uncle in North Carolina, and then traveling north over "roads deep under snow or slippery with ice," until he met a group of travelers who were taking a ferry across thin ice on the frigid Susquehanna on their way to Philadelphia. He arrived at his father's house in January and was pleased to find his mother and father still alive.

The fruits of his labors over the last four years were sent in boxes to his patron, Lord Fothergill, in England.

He came home to his father's farm and garden at Kingsessing and lived there for almost forty more years. In 1805 he turned down an offer from Jefferson to lead an expedition up the Red River. He was too old, he said. And declined an invitation from the University of Pennsylvania to be a professor. He was a gardener from the time he rode up to his father's house in the winter of 1777 until he died in July 1823 just after taking his morning stroll in the garden.

His journey covered the wild parts of the Carolinas and Georgia, retracing a route he and his father had taken on their trip to Florida in 1765–66 when his father had been appointed King's Botanist. He rediscovered the plant his father named Franklinia and gathered seeds that he planted in his garden at home when he returned. He spent months in the mountains of Georgia and the Carolinas and explored the western part of Florida with a party of traders and land speculators.

Before his expedition, he had failed at being a merchant and a settler. He was in debt. His attempt to start a rice plantation near the St. Johns River in East Florida left him broke and despondent. In April 1766, before heading home, his father had supplied him money and sent "4 good yams two white & two red," writing, "A rice barrel . . . one covered pot, one iron pot, one heavy pensylvania ax . . . Captain hardy did bring thy watch to be mended & took away to Philadelphia—promised to leave it with thy mother." He also left good millstones and a grindstone, a pair of smoothing irons, and a long list of things that William would need to start a rice plantation on the wild banks of the wide St. Johns.

John's instructions to William for planting rice are to set fire "to the 20 acre marsh . . . if it be two wett hoe it up in narrow ridges & plant the rice on the ridge for all agree if the water covers the young blade it will kill it." Peter Collinson thought he needed "a Virtuous Industrious Wife such as knows how to share the Toils as well as the Comforts of a Marriage State."

Bartram also bought for his son six slaves: Jack and his wife, Siby; Jacob and Sam; and Flora and her son Bachus, "a pretty boy" who was about four years old. I have a hard time reading John Bartram's letter to his son that lists the supplies he has procured. He is worried about Billy. He's asked for advice from his friends about which slaves to buy, like purchasing a pot or an ax, but much more important because these six people will be the ones to make the plantation habitable and profitable.

I wonder about Flora and her young son. Bartram had chosen her as a wife for Jacob. By the time Henry Laurens, a friend of the Bartrams, visited William in July, only two of the men could handle an ax to help clear the swamp at his settlement. He had not yet planted rice in July.

In August, Henry Laurens wrote a letter to John Bartram describing William's health after a summer on his plantation:

> His situation on the river is the least agreeable of all the places that I have seen,—on a low sheet of sandy pine barren, verging on the swamp, which before his door is very narrow, in a bight or cove of the river . . . the water almost stagnated, exceedingly foul, and absolutely stank when stirred up by our oars.

His crops are stunted, his house "a hovel, that he lives in, is extremely confined, and not proof against the weather." His provisions are "scanty"; his health is "imperfect."

> Possibly, sir, your son, though a worthy, ingenious man, may not have resolution, or not that sort of resolution, that is necessary to encounter the difficulties incident to, and unavoidable in his present state of life.

William, he writes, "had felt the pressure of his solitary and hopeless condition so heavily, as almost to drive him to despondency."

By 1767 he was home at his father's farm in Kingsessing. And Collinson writes, "It Grieves Mee Much to hear of Poor Billys adversity but I hope his Virtuous Mind will support him under it."

Not long after, he fled south to his uncle's farm in North Carolina to escape a creditor who threatened to kill him. Before he left he had been sending drawings to Peter Collinson who then sold them to several English collectors. Dr. John Fothergill, a Quaker and a physician in London, sometimes physician to the crown, was a friend of Collinson and admired William's work. He had a famous garden in Essex, financed natural history expeditions and publications, and found plants for Kew Gardens. After Collinson's death in August 1768 he wrote to John, "I called upon my Friend one morning this summer, when he showed me some exquisite drawings of thy son's. He proposed that I should engage thy son to make drawings of all your land tortoises."

When William returned from North Carolina, after his father settled his debts, Fothergill became William's patron. He accepted Bartram's proposal that he would explore Florida for one or two years and send his drawings and botanical discoveries to Fothergill.

William Bartram was an inspired explorer and artist. His vision, when he finally composed his book many years after his trip, was of a world shinning with "an amazing display of the wisdom and power of the supreme author of nature." He argued for the protection of the Creek and Cherokee villages he visited. His version of the world was democratic and included all the tribes he described as finny or furred as well as human: "The animal creation also excites our admiration, and equally manifests the almighty power, wisdom, and beneficence of the Supreme Creator and Sovereign Lord of the universe; some in their vast size and strength, as the mammoth, the elephant, the whale, the lion, and alligator; others in their beauty and elegance of colour, plumage, and rapidity of flight, having the faculty of moving and living in the air."

The Alachua savanna in northern Florida was one of the places he admired. He described the "level green plain" in his book as being "fifty miles in circumference, and scarcely a tree or bush of any kind to be seen on it. It is encircled with high, sloping hills, covered with waving forests and fragrant Orange groves, rising from exuberantly fertile soil. The towering magnolia grandiflora and transcendent Palm, stand conspicuous amongst them."

There were "innumerable droves of cattle" and "herds of sprightly deer, squadrons of the beautiful fleet Siminole horse, flocks of turkeys, civilized communities of the sonorous watchful crane." He called the savanna and a little lake nearby filled with golden blossoms the "borders of a new world."

Bartram's drawing of the savanna is a vision of a miraculous place. The trunk of a royal palm anchors the left of the picture, and groves of oranges and magnolias and pines cluster in regular procession around the watery interior. Deer and cranes and horses, all the same size, frolic at the edges of the marshy streams. Near the palm a crane bends her head to the left under a tall lily. The scene is ordered and rhythmic. There's a tiny wooden structure near a pond filled with water lilies.

He shared a dinner one night of a savanna crane with an eight-foot wingspan: "When these birds move their wings in flight, their strokes are slow, moderate, and regular: and even, when at a considerable distance or high above us, we plainly hear the quill-feathers, their shafts and webs upon one another creak as the joints or working of a vessel in a tempestuous sea."

"It made excellent soup," he thought, "nevertheless, as long as I can get any other necessary food, I shall prefer their seraphic music in the ethereal skies."

He became a friend of a powerful chief, called Cowkeeper, of the Creek village of Cuscowilla, who gave him the name of "Puc-Puggy" or the Flower Hunter.

In the Carolinas he climbed a steep ridge with a trader to look down on "a vast expanse of green meadows and strawberry fields." There was a "gliding" river and Cherokee girls gathering strawberries, their faces and lips stained with the fruit. Some of the young women were lying on the riverbank, dipping their hands into the water. "Nature prevailing over reason," he explains in his *Travels*, "we wished at least to have a more active part in their delicious sports."

He and his friend crept down the hill and surprised the girls and the women who were watching them. They were given a basket of ripe berries and sat down to eat the fruit surrounded by the girls and the "elder matrons."

"By concessions and suitable apologies for the bold intrusion," his young companion arranged to buy the berries and have the women bring their harvest to his house.

Bartram trotted across fields of berries, the ankles of his horse red with the juice.

How could you just ride home after all this?

In March 1775 he sent his father a letter:

Honord & Benevolent Father

I am happy by the blessing of the Almighty God by whose care I have been protected & led safe through a Pilgrimage these three & twenty months till my return to Charlestown two days since.

He explains that he is "lodged" with the family of John's friend Lambol. "I collected," he writes, "a large number of specimens & sent to Doctr Fothergill with some drawings in answer to which the Doctr was pleased to send me a list of the new & nondescript which I was glad to find were many, & hear he was pleased to express his satisfaction with the success of my labours & his willingness that I should continue my researches."

His travels had been dictated by the "hostilities commencing" between the Indians and the settlers on the frontier, stirred up by the British.

His parents had not heard from him for two years. Bartram traveled to the Mississippi on one of the last parts of his long journey in the Southeast. He rode west from Florida to the very mouth of the river. In his book, *Travels Through North and South Carolina,*

*Georgia, East and West Florida, The Cherokee Country, The Extensive Territories of the Muscogulges, or Creek Confederacy, And the Country of the Chactaws,* he describes riding across a land swept clear of the remnants of old villages. He passes deserted settlements, ghosts of towns filled with groves of gleaming orange trees and the traces of once cultivated fields. The flourishing strawberry fields and fruitful gardens of the Cherokee Indians in the Carolinas were destroyed soon after he stood at the top of the ridge looking down on the girls picking fruit. Settlers burned the fragrant flowers and sweet fields of strawberries in retaliation for the Cherokee's alliance with the British.

In 1775 he paddled around the shallow rivers of Mobile in August and came down with a fever so severe he "expected to sink under the malady." He went thirty miles upriver to find a plant he was convinced could cure him. He was partially blinded by this illness and had trouble with his eyes off and on after this fever.

After four or five weeks doctored by "an English gentleman who had a variety of medicines" and who lived on an island near Mobile, Bartram recovered his sight and traveled to the Mississippi. He writes, "The depth of the river here, even in this season, at its lowest ebb, is astonishing, not less than forty fathoms; and the width about a mile or somewhat less: but it is not expansion of surface alone that strikes us with ideas of magnificence; the altitude and theatrical ascents of its pensile banks, the steady course of the mighty flood, the trees, high forests, every particular object, as well as societies, bear the stamp of superiority and excellence; all unite or combine in exhibiting a prospect of the grand sublime."

This was as far west as he would travel.

Edward Cashin, in his book *William Bartram and the American Revolution on the Southern Frontier,* writes that in 1776 Bartram was involved in an attempt to stop an invasion by the British at St. Augustine into Georgia at St. Marys. Lachlan McIntosh and volunteers, including his friend William Bartram, stationed themselves under the trees on the banks of the St. Marys and shot at the British who were attacking along with their Indian allies from the ruins of an Indian trading house on the other side of the river. The Indians were Creeks fighting under their chief, Ahaya, who turned out to be Bartram's friend Cowkeeper of Cuscowilla. Upon seeing Bartram, Cowkeeper threw down his gun and walked to the riverbank, where the mud was being spattered by bullets. He told the men from Georgia that they were brothers and friends and he wouldn't fire another shot. He then turned and led his men away.

At the end of his *Travels*, Bartram complains for the first and only time of being alone and tired. He gives up his cherished faithful horse and buys a new one. On the way back from the Mississippi he describes his delight at seeing Great Springs again near Savannah: "This amazing fountain of transparent cool water, breaks suddenly out of the earth at the basis of a moderately elevated hill or bank forming, at once a bason near twenty yards over . . . The ebbulition is copious, active and continual over the ragged apertures in the rocks, which lie seven or eight feet below . . . There are multitudes of fish in the fountain, of various tribes, chiefly the several species of bream, trout, cat-fish, and garr: it was amusing to behold the fish continually ascending and descending through the rocky apertures."

"Magnolia grandiflora, Laurus Borbonia, Quercus sempervirens, Callicarpa; at a little distance, a grove of the Cassine; and in an old field, just by, are to be seen some small Indian mounts." A glimpse of paradise for readers in Philadelphia or London who were accustomed to more cultivated gardens.

His last chapters are a record of the Indian nations he visited. He argues that the government should reform Indian policy. In the *Travels* he loses track of time and rearranges the order of his expeditions.

His narrative doesn't mention the Revolution, or the burned towns, or the deserted fields.

Once home it took many years before the book was finished. He paid off his last creditors. He reworked his book and completed a draft in 1786. He fell out of a tree while collecting seeds, not long after, and fractured his right leg. He spent a year close to death. When he was well he finished a series of fifty-nine drawings he had started for Fothergill, who had died in 1780, and mounted the last specimens from his travels. He sent them off to Robert Barclay and Sir Joseph Banks, the naturalist and explorer who was involved in the development of the Royal Botanic Gardens at Kew. Banks never catalogued Bartram's discoveries. The book was not published until 1791.

# 20. *Wild Rice*

FOUR OR FIVE GREAT BLUE HERONS live in the shallows of Darby Creek in the John Heinz National Wildlife Refuge at Tinicum, another wild garden in Philadelphia. The tide is out so the water is low and brown. We're surrounded by the grays and browns of late winter—things are still held within themselves here in the marsh. It's cold and the wind puts a blush on my son's cheeks and makes my husband huddle under his hat.

We're not far from Bartram's Garden here. Darby Creek and its freshwater tidal marsh is the last bit of the vast marsh that covered this part of the city hundreds of years ago.

The herons are slender and dusky at the bend of the creek on its way to the Delaware. They're wading around the dark shapes of black ducks bobbing on the low water at the bend. From up the creek we saw a muskrat slip into the water from the smooth muddy bank, a muscular shape in the dark water. We can now see her prints in the mud.

I've read that in winter the muskrat is trapped for its fur. In the silky green marshes along the Delaware south of Philadelphia, trappers put out steel traps at the entrance of the muskrats' burrows, silvery thatched huts that stick up above the surface of the marsh. Bruce Stutz writes that the muskrat crawls or swims through the steel wicket, catches the lever, releases the bail, and is stunned or killed, caught in the trap. In 1864, three million muskrat pelts were sold in the United States, making the muskrat the most trapped animal in North America. Colonists and Europeans used the strong musk extracted from muskrat glands to perfume their beds and their bodies and their clothes.

A healthy marsh can support fifty muskrats per acre. The female has three or more litters per year and spends the winter huddled in "a many chambered burrow." They like to eat cattails, bulrushes, wild rice, river willow, and sometimes fish and crayfish. Their hind feet are weblike, with a ridge of stiff hairs.

We pass many intricate nests poised in the bare branches of the rangy trees. One delicate oriole nest hangs above the path like a lace bag. All are empty now but we know that soon they'll be filled with life. Eighty species of birds nest here. I think about the Baltimore oriole's winter life, her tropical nature. Scott Weidensaul in his book *Living on the Wind* describes orioles in the wet forests of northern Belize, sipping nectar from the white blossoms of bribri trees. We think of the oriole and other songbirds as part of our landscape, but really, Weidensaul writes, they're just as much inhabitants of more exotic places, spending almost seven months in their nonbreeding range in Mexico or as far south as Colombia, with toucans and parakeets for neighbors.

When orioles fly north they're part of the vast migration that sweeps across the earth in spring and again in fall. Weidensaul tells me that researchers know that migrating birds "can track the sun, the moon, and the stars, compensating for their apparent movement to use them as compasses. But birds can also apparently perceive a host of sensations that are beyond our unaided senses—weak magnetic fields, faint odors, polarized light, barometric pressure, even extraordinary low-frequency sound waves that echo halfway around the world."

Wind shapes their paths. Above us at night in fall thousands of birds fly south over Philadelphia on their way to Mexico, Brazil, and Patagonia. Most birds migrate at night when the air is cooler. If I knew what I was looking at, I could stand on my deck in late September and count the orioles or herons flying south as their silhouettes pass in front of the burning moon.

This time of year flocks of robins fly up our street and peck the red berries off door swags and wreaths. I saw a large robin yesterday nipping the last berry on my neighbor's pine and holly swag, the bird's beak stuck up under the striped bow. In Maine this time of year the birds eat winterberries, cold and bright red.

William Bartram kept careful records of the migration of birds. His notations on the pages of small bound notebooks, now fallen apart, welcomed flocks of birds as friends from the fall returned in the spring. His father described the migration of "hooping cranes" in a letter to Peter Collinson in January 1757: "in their passage from florida to Hudson bay thay fly in flocks . . . so exceeding high as scarcely to be observed but by thair perticular noise of thair loud hooping we can but just see them."

The brown cattails and phragmites and wild rice of the marsh bristle with cold. In a couple of months, carp will spawn in the warm, shallow water. Somewhere church bells are ringing. All along the edge of the marsh stand the huge round tanks of an oil company.

## 21. Bloodroot

I'VE BEEN WALKING IN THE VALLEY of the Wissahickon, down the steep paths to where the stream meanders through its course, pooling at the site of old mill ponds and then rushing and splitting over the rocks that tumbled down a long time ago. It's the thick of spring, and I'm amazed that I recognize the faces of flowers from many years ago when I wandered the woods near our house in Vermont, up the steep sides of the mountain, down the cool valleys of the little brooks, through the grassy meadows to a cliff where I used to sit and look out toward the Connecticut River Valley.

I'm making a list in my head as I walk along the river on a narrow path through the tulip trees and hemlocks that tower five stories above me, budded and bursting as the air warms. Adder's tongue, hepatica, purple violets, fiddleheads unfurling, shadblow, mountain anemone, starflowers, spring beauties, Solomon's seal, trout lilies, the shiny fat leaves of rhododendron. The stark white flowers of bloodroot. The flower closes at night, snapped shut against its single scalloped leaf. The dark red sap of its underground stem was used three hundred years ago as a dye for war paint and baskets and clothing. The Latin genus name—*Sanguinaria*—means "bleeding."

It's ten miles to Fair Mount from here. I saw a marker on the gravel road called Forbidden Drive. I'm weightless here—the past, mine and the woods, thrown off in the exuberant now of spring. It's a cliché again but I like it. I mourn my father in other seasons. I touch the very tips of my husband's long fingers as we walk. Our son is on the plateau above us a mile or so back playing tennis. We're not springlike ourselves but pretend to be blossoming like all the old trees around us. They've done this thing for over two hundred years or so. Why is it so hard for us to unfurl and luxuriate in the early warmth?

I'm convinced John Bartram and Ann Bartram loved each other through their long marriage. The only surviving letter to her was written when John and his son William, or Billy, as his family called him, traveled to Florida after John Bartram was appointed King's Botanist:

Savannah September the 4th 1765

My dear Spouse

This day we arrived at Savanna town in georgia by 10 oclock this was reconed A very hot day here with thunder & showers thermometer 86 they have had here as well as at Charles town the hottest summer & dryest; & wettest August that hath been for many years many great bridges is broken down & we were forced to swim our horses over but God all mighty be praised we are got safe into Georgia & strange it is that in all this dreadful season for thunder & prodigious rain we have not had occation to put A great coat on in both the Carolinas nor rested one day on the account of rain but we cant expect to be favoured so long; however Gods will be done: we are now hearty & has A good stomack the people say that if we can weather this month we need not fear: we have been pestered these two mornings & evenings with very large muskitos but thair bite is not near so venemous as the small sort at Charles town: the land in general is pretty good most of the way from Charles town to this town & the people very civil to us . . .

we are obliged to be at or near Augustine by the first of october or thereabouts so that we have but about A month to travel 500 miles in

My dear love: my love is to all our children & friends as if perticularly named which I have not time nor room at present to do & and its by the Governours favour as well as information that I met with this opertunity to deliver it to his care in A letter to Mr. Lambol

our Son Billy I hope if we have our health will be of great service to me he desires to be remembered to his mother, brothers, sisters & friends

September ye 5th.—Thermo 80 just ready to set out toward augusta when we have breakfasted perhaps the next letter may be dated from Augustine; but if we come back to this town we shall be for writing here.

however dear love in the mean time I remain thy affectionate husband,

John Bartram in grat hast

this town is pretily situate on dry sandy ground & generaly good water great ships ly close too & safe harbour

After the deaths of William Bartram's mother and father, he lived in the house at Kingsessing with his brother John and his family. And he referred to himself as a bachelor reluctantly. One of his biographers, Thomas Slaughter, thinks he might have been in love with his cousin Mary. When he was almost fifty, two years after his fall and convalescence, he wrote: "Cousin, don't doubt my assertion, when I tell you that time, vicissitudes of fortune, tribulation, I may say indeed, the decrepitude of old age, are not sufficient to erase from my mind those impressions which it received during my residence in my uncle's family in North Carolina."

I'm wondering about love this morning. And thinking about love and gardens. I was nineteen when I went to Oxford to spend the year. I turned twenty in January. I had no idea what love was. I thought soon that I was in love with another American who was not very tall and had a thick beard and sensuous lips and came from Oregon. I had never been in a place more beautiful than Oxford, with its meadows spread out along the banks of narrow rivers, cows nibbling the long sweet grass, or the cobbled streets of the city, or the walled gardens near my flat. I often walked through the parks at dusk, my long jean skirt hitting the brick walks with a swish. In March I went south to the mild coast of Cornwall and saw gardens filled with daffodils and large-leaved plants as big as golf umbrellas.

I wandered around my neighborhood at dusk, putting my face into the full-throated bloom of the pink and yellow and red roses pushed up against fences in the small, neat front yards of my invisible neighbors. I wanted to know about sex but wasn't brave enough to try anything with my friend from Oregon. Sometimes we would go out to a dock on the river at night and kiss by the side of the silent water. I could smell the perfume of night flowers, the heavy roses as I kissed the lips of this American. One night I climbed the fence of the locked parks with an older Englishman, a son of a woman who lived across the street from my flat in an old stable. He was much more dangerous than Andy and I was afraid of seeing him again.

Sometimes in the spring I made cakes with a friend who came to live with me, decorated with the pink petals of roses and the sweet faces of pansies. It seemed daring to eat flowers.

Now I take my husband's hand, curl my fist in the length of his palm. The bright waxy petals of the bloodroot poke up in the leaf litter of countless seasons.

# 22. *Shadblow*

WE'RE HEADING UPRIVER on the green silky water of a ghost river. We don't know it as we chug northwest in our motored barge, but near the shore in the shallow water of the Schuylkill there's a body floating. I'm thinking about all the boats that were here when the Bartrams lived on their farm. All the commerce and activity that churned up the shallow waters. Now it's as if we're on a wilderness trip, slowly making our way past the broken spires of mountains and the clogged hearts of rivers and bays. But we're traveling instead through the years on the river, past rotting pilings, iron structures for trains and power plants, an old motel perched on the very edge of the west bank where men lean out of windows and shout at us as we head back down the river. Our captain takes us to the waterworks below the art museum. They're on the edge of the river, too, the miniature buildings from the early 1800s newly painted with a creamy yellow that stands out against the cliff behind them, the first spine of the Piedmont, lifting itself up from the coastal plain.

Graham and Scott lean out over the prow of the square barge. I bend to look straight ahead into the future. Our guide is telling us that soon there'll be a dock at Bartram's garden, soon these trips will be commonplace. Now, we're the only boat on the lower river. Fishermen and young boys with sticks wave at us from the east bank. We pass a goose on a nest in the splinters of railroad ties.

All the new leaves of the trees and bushes of the riverbank shimmer in the early-afternoon light, chilled and expectant. The air is sweet on the river—spring—smelling of blooming. Cormorants and geese and crows and seagulls fly up or down as we circle to the fall line and back. In the bushes by Bartrams' field I see the flash of an oriole and hear a cardinal whistling his territory. Maybe there's a kingfisher chattering there, too. A man in a bow tie and a straw hat has come for the ride. And a woman who takes notes for the newspaper, her arm wrapped around the large arm of her companion, a man with glinting chains around his neck.

"I'll be sure to put all this in the piece," she says to Bill LeFevre, the director of Bartram's Garden.

We could be anywhere but here on the river in the city. I'm sipping wine. I'm thinking about Ann Bartram and her wagon crossing the floating bridge that's no longer here at Grays Ferry, taking her butter to market.

# 23. The Lady Petre Pear Tree

THERE'S A WIDE GRAVELED WALK edged in ivy. It's 1890 or so. The pear tree is half dead and very large against the white sky— luminous on the postcard. The edge of the seed house faces the garden. Other spiky branches spread their limbs in the air. You can't see the house John Bartram built in the photograph. It's hidden.

I'm trying to think about the grace of the pear tree, the history of the garden, the countless letters sent back and forth on ships between John Bartram and his friend Peter Collinson. And Ann Bartram's last years in the house.

The soil in the garden and fields that John Bartram once owned has been cultivated for a long time. Archeologists have found artifacts from 3000 BC through 1000 AD: a "triangular jasper point" and shards of prehistoric bowls in the fields near the bend in the river.

Excavations in the area of the "New Garden" on William Bartram's drawing unearthed straight paths with cobble edging and a surface of "gravely-clay soil." Under the grass were planting holes with six inches of black soil, soot from the industrial city of the late nineteenth century. Beds cultivated to a depth of four feet were discovered below the top layers of soil, part of the botanic garden from 1760 to 1850.

The pear tree, ancient when the Bartram Association made the postcard in 1890, first bore fruit around 1763, and a pear from the tree may be a prop in a painting that is thought to be of John Bartram. Lord Petre was one of Bartram's first and most enthusiastic collectors and a great friend of Peter Collinson. He was an English Catholic. When he died at thirty, Collinson wrote to Bartram, "I have lost my

Friend, my brother, the man I Loved & was dearer to Mee than all men, is no more."

A year before Lord Petre's death in 1742 from smallpox, Collinson writes, "the Trees and shrubbs raised from thy first seeds is grown to great maturity Last year Ld petre planted out about Tenn thousand Americans wch being att the Same Time mixed with about twenty Thousand Europeans, & some Asians make a very beautiful appearance great Art and & skill being shown in consulting Every one's pticular growth & the well blending the Variety of Greens."

In October, 1763 Bartram writes to Collinson, "I am heartily glad that young Lord Petre is posesed of the Botanical genius of his father I wish he may in vertue too I have intended to have inquired after him & and his mother in every last letter the pear raised from her seed hath bore here A number of the finest relished fruite that I think A better is not in the world & intend next spring to graft several of them."

Other cards have pieces of the house or the garden: a window open to the river breeze, curtains parted just a bit; a photograph of a Franklinia bloom, five white petals fluted at the ends, the anthers like pompom frills, bright orange; two tall boxwood trees, very old on the south side of the house; a rain barrel; twisted ivy on the stout pillars of the porch facing the river; a yellowwood tree.

The garden is quiet in these photographs, there is simply no one here.

# 24. *Zinnia*

SHOOTS THE COLOR OF FRESH RHUBARB STALKS are thrusting up from the cut branches of our two rose bushes. I pulled off the Christmas greens from the soil this morning. Poked around the cinnamon fern. Fiddleheads are crouched at the base of the fruiting frond, a brown branch with tight brown leaves that weathered the winter. I dug this fern and another, a royal fern, from the woods near my mother's house in Vermont. Their cool green wildness survived the heat this summer in a low pot. In the fall I transplanted them to the small garden bed that divides my tiny patio from my neighbor George's back yard.

Our pots survived the winter. We wrapped the terra-cotta urns in bubble wrap and clustered the other pots together in the sheltered patio. I read this morning that a potter in Connecticut makes pots based on shards from Colonial gardens. He has one pot that's fashioned from a chip of pottery found at Bartram's garden.

There's no grass growing in our small garden, but the sage is sprouting little tufts of gray leaves, the narcissus pop their light green leaves up through the woodchips, the holly trees glow with warm rain, ivy stretches along the fence.

In the long bed that lines the side of the house along the sidewalk there are rustlings, too. Irises are slicing the soil.

I'm thinking about a swamp sparrow, all his body singing, throat to tail feathers vibrating with the song, repeated and repeated until another sparrow answers. I watched him for a long time this morning and then walked home. My ferns are unfurling as the shad swim hard upriver through the fish ladder to the end of the city.

Scott interviewed for his job on a very hot dry day in the early summer a couple of years ago. We drove south from Massachusetts through the Meadowlands over the bridge from New Jersey to the center of the city. We'd been living in a green place where flocks of wild turkeys spent the winter in our backyard. Beavers lived down the street in a marsh. In spring deer nibbled the tips of my tulip leaves. That first day the city was a blast of hot air and noise, the shiny glare of summer. I couldn't catch my breath. We felt buffeted by heat and exhaust and the screech of car tires.

But the next day we found the garden. It was not far from where Scott would be working and where Graham would go to school. In the large square next to The Franklin Institute, I touched the tips of fruiting grasses and Queen Anne's lace and we sat on painted metal benches. Graham fiddled with contraptions—speaking tubes and floating stone globes. I saw little sparrows hanging from the tips of daisies and the buds of beach roses. It smelled like summer.

Now, as I write, women gather near the parking lot at St. Francis Xavier School. They've walked two blocks west and stand in the bright windy chill waiting for their children to run around the corner of the school. They're speaking Spanish. I gave my Spanish textbook away. I still have a Norwegian grammar and a first-year Greek book. Somewhere I have a Welsh dictionary and a Lappish children's book. I'm not good at languages.

Soon my child will hop off his yellow school bus. And I'm thinking about Italy. I'm lusting after a life in Italy. I'm thinking about lemons and cream and new tomatoes, hot in the hand.

A version of cabin fever. I try not to worry about the quality of the air here. I admire the white caps on the river. I make a note that the buses are coming down the street again and two red-tailed hawks are hunting over Lemon Hill. I want too many things. I make a note to consider what I have.

I long to plant vegetables I can eat, little fat lettuces and shiny grapes. Thin bright orange carrots and hot rough artichokes, sweet peppers and long firm corn.

We don't know for sure what's in the soil at the community garden. One man told Scott the soil was thick with something called Philadelphia ash. Anne Whiston Spirn tells me in her book *The Granite Garden*, "Soil is the crust of the earth in which life is rooted—a porous medium between rock and air. It is neither entirely mineral nor entirely organic; it is composed of sand, silt, clay, air, water and the decomposed remains of plants and animals."

I think about the soil in our plot, its soft, silty feel on my hand. Sometimes I see men peeing in the bamboo grove near our plants. Several cats who live in the garden scratch around the delicate leaves of lettuce.

I've been reading about earthworms this morning. An article in the newspaper reports that earthworms didn't exist in the northern half of the eastern United States until they were introduced by European settlers. The line of native earthworms indicated how far the glaciers advanced south. The soil is different where earthworms are absent, more leafy, less chewed and digested. We're at the southern edge of a glaciated landscape here, so the native earthworms have been doing their job in the soil of the community garden for a very long time.

When I dig my shovel into the soil I flip the layers of time over and over again: the heavy soil of the Piedmont, the vanished traces of tulip trees and chestnuts, the bodies of slippery worms and beetles with shiny purple backs, the bricks of the houses that were once here ground into pink powder, a layer of Philadelphia ash, soot from the factories that once surrounded this area, leaves from our elms, a layer of composted manure. I'm cultivating some of the same elements that the Bartrams plowed on their farm.

Cities, Spirn tells me, are "fragile creations balanced on the earth's crust, exposed to the slow but inexorable pace of erosion and sedimentation, vulnerable to every tremor of the violent forces beneath, and dependent upon dwindling mineral resources."

I like thinking about the garden's breath, how plants suck their drink from the ground and then exhale water into the air. There's always water circulating on the globe, I read not long ago in E. C. Pielou's book *Fresh Water*. Water has no beginning and no end. We're cooled by the vapor of the plants and trees in the city. Some of our water comes from "'snowballs' of nearly pure snow, the size of small houses . . . entering the earth's gravity field from the outer parts of the solar system every few seconds."

Under our feet, there's water, too, hidden in solid ground, fossil water, buried in rocks. Water that falls on the garden as rain, or is poured on, seeps into the soil that's filled with curled and spiny and delicate organisms that twist and bend and curl, poking holes in the soil for the water.

My three elm trees survive against all odds, their roots under soil that's paved over and filled in with foundations. The only loose soil is at their base where I've planted small gardens. The elms breathe, cool on the hottest days here. Drinking their water from far below the street, building their tissues with nutrients from the soil and sweating the rest of the water into the hot air. They could be drinking from one of the streams that disappeared under the city. More than fifty threads of water—creek or rivulet, brook, or stream—flowed into the Schuylkill when Penn arrived. They vanished within one hundred years.

The water I gather at the spigot is Schuylkill River water, flowing water that started at a tiny seep and collected enough force to erode the soil into a channel, a small brook that joined with other small streams and flowed down into a valley and then a river where threads of water continually slide past each other.

"A river's surface is usually a narrow strip of the water table exposed above ground," Pielou writes.

I wonder about the way we slip through the lives of past cultivation. So little exposed above the ground.

I decide to grow a cutting garden, long stems of bright zinnias, once an exotic from Mexico, now their feet balanced in the ancient soil of the city, drinking water recycled from the gods.

# 25. Snowdrops

JANUARY 15, 1802, was "clear and as warm as May day no ice to be seen in the river etc bees out till evening flying about sparrow hawk & Blew bird. crocus verna. Narsissus. snowdrops Tuleps. Above ground. Hamamelis. In full bloom. Wind S. W."

I know the weather for twenty years, a list of familiar birds, the opening petals of winter aconite, the swelling of peach buds, the misty sky, the mild sun, the shiny moon, sultry days and the fields drying up or wet Julys where the hay rotted. I know that some summer nights were so dark with thunder that William Bartram noted that the candles were lit to dine. I know there was a little owl who came back year after year.

Each time I read his carefully written diary I know a bit more about what he saw in those two last decades of his long life. I could chart each day from January 1, 1802, until December 31, 1822. He died in his garden in July 1823.

December 1802 was

generally moderate weather. White frost in the morning & warm pleasant day or moderate showers, clearing at N. W. & after, frost enough to scale over shallow ponds with Ice, which was melted before night. till 16th when clearing up from N. W. after a warm rainy day became extreme cold; & the night of the 17th. froze Schuylkill completely over. 18th people were sporting on the Ice of the Delaware & Schuylkill. 20th moderate. 23rd the Ice broke up & by the 25th no Ice to be seen. About this time a very small owl was caught not much exceeding the size of a sparrow. (Capitae laevi) from this time to the end of the month moderate weather, a slight fall of snow & Schuylkill scaled over with Ice, but disappear'd next day.

Sometimes January was mild—"serene and as warm as the month of May after a white frosty morning"—in other years Bartram recorded three inches of new snow "on old snow on the earth."

Frogs sang on one January day in a "thawy wind." A little horned owl was hunting mice about the house. Large flights of crows to the south. The river was full of flocks of ducks.

January 6 was a pleasant day in 1804, the evening hazy and warm. Bartram noted "Mockbird, Blue bird Robbin Flicca. Meadowlark. Falco sparverius. Dandelion in Flower as well as Violets, Veronica, Hab Robert, & some others." Later in the month purple finches were feeding on the seeds of the ash.

In 1812 China roses bloomed in the greenhouse and "magnolia conspicua" with a "flower 7½ inches expansion."

There was a snowy winter in 1821, with eighteen inches of snow in early January.

In February the "snow birds begin to associate, meditating their departure for the north." People filled their ice houses and woodcocks arrived from the south.

"Spiders dart their Webbs, Peach Trees begin to assume a redish colour in the last years Growth, & their blossom-buds begin to swell."

When I look out the window in the room where I write, it's March, almost spring but not quite. We've just had snow, an inch or so of wet spring snow that's bent the snowdrops down in the little garden bed behind the house and coated the daffodils on the side. I met a man yesterday who told me that in Florida where his family lived they would put heaters out near the orange trees to keep them warm in this kind of weather. You could stand in the field and feel the heat on your skin but none of it ever touched the trees. He has land in Mississippi but doesn't want to go back there. They don't know how to behave there, he told me. He said the fruit trees might be hit here, the buds frozen on their icy twigs. I liked talking about weather, waiting in the cold for the bus. I couldn't remember what month it was for a second. And the wind felt like a north wind, icy and sharp, bitter in the mouth.

The silver maple down the street is full of red buds, and the extravagant and ancient fritillaria is poking up in the side bed. The bulbs smelled like a skunk and were covered with sawdust from the supplier.

The Carolina chickadee who lives in a hole in the sycamore tree sits on the branch of the elm outside my bedroom and sings to me. The finches clear the feeder of all the sunflower hearts.

In Bartram's garden the snowdrops (*Galanthus vernus*) were in flower on March 10 in 1802, and they bloomed on March 18 in 1803. Some Februarys were mild enough for seeds to sprout in the open ground. He lists radish and larkspur and "many in flower." In December 1802 many "seeds vegetate in the open garden, as Larkspurs, Honesty, Acuba Japonia, Lylicium Europium, Peryploca greca Virginian silk, Fumaria fungosa, Fumaria glauca, Denetheria fruticosa, Solanium Marginatum."

I figure the weather was warmer then than it is now, which seems strange. My seeds would rot if I planted them in the garden in December. Maybe I've misunderstood his notation, maybe they were in the greenhouse or were seeds that needed a winter to germinate. I wonder if Bartram planted the seeds himself or another member of the family scattered the tiny seeds and pushed them into the soil. During this time William was running the family business with his brother John and lived with John's family in their father's house. He had a pet crow called Tom that followed him out to the garden and watched him as he wrote in his study or slept under a peach tree.

When he was weeding in the garden his companion, he wrote, "would often fly to me, and, after very attentively observing me in pulling up the small weeds and grass, he would fall to work, and with his strong beak, pluck up the grass; and more so, when I complimented him with encouraging expressions."

Bartram wrote articles and illustrated natural history books. At some point he drafted a speech against slavery on the back of a copy of the Bartram garden catalog of 1783 to read to the new government in Philadelphia.

The kingfisher arrived from the south on March 22 one year, and in another March a man was found frozen to death. On the nineteenth he saw the "Aurora borialis," and shad and herring were brought to market. The skunk cabbage flowered.

One April the peach trees began to bloom. In 1812, April was cold: "Frost with Ice, cold Blustering wind NW, House wren arived, Bluebird and domestic Sparrow lay Eggs."

*Acer saccharinum* was in bloom, swarming with bees sucking nectar from the flowers. A cold rain washed the flowers of blue violets and early yellow violets, *Dentaria enneaphylla, Claytonia virginica, Ranunculus sylvestris,* and trillium in 1802. The wild tulip bloomed.

On April 3 in 1803 it was "warm growing weather . . . Husband Men sowing spring-Barly & planting early potatoes. Flax & Hemp above ground. pasture grounds assume a pleasing green livery." By the fourth, shad were caught in great abundance. The fishing hawk arrived from the south on the twenty-ninth.

On the eighteenth of April in 1818 he recorded the death of his nephew: "Cool wind high, blustering from NW. N.B. died this morning Dr. James Bartram of Kingsess, grandson of the celebrated John Bartram the Botanist & naturalist."

In 1822 on the twenty-fifth it was as hot as midsummer, the thermometer at eighty-two at noon. One April "buildings were set on fire by lightening and burnt."

May was misty sometimes with a morning wind and cruel with cold rains for a week "injurious to vegitation and to the farmers. Wheat just begining to ear appears to be blasted in many instances," and young birds drowned in their nests on the ground.

Now and then Bartram's notations look different, smaller script, less detail. In the last year he kept the diary his writing scrawls across one page as if his hand slipped.

The green twig whortleberry is in flower on May 6 in 1802, and the next May he records that a bullfrog swallowed a large mole instantly. That May there was a hard frost on the seventh that killed the young shoots of trees and shrubs. In the last year of the diary on May 13 there were "numerous tribes of small birds, feeding on the aphids on the apple, pear trees—towhe bunting building their nests in the garden."

In 1819 early in May, the bluebirds brought out their first brood "which are under the protection of the father whilst the hen is laying for the next family."

It's April here now and I'm hardening off my young shoots and slips of bushes on the deck off the bedroom. Tender greens of monarda and *Clethra alnifolia*, the dark narrow leaves of tiarella and amsonia, tight buds of violas. After about a week I'll plant them in the little garden bed on the patio, my woodland garden. I'm hoping we won't get a hard frost in May, though the directions for my plants tell me to throw a row cover or some mulch over the new shoots if frost is predicted.

Right now the *Erythronium americanum* 'Pagoda' is just about to bloom, yellow dogtooth violets. And the leaves of the wood poppy are unfurling. If I poke my finger into the soil I can see the hard green curls of fiddleheads hidden just below the surface. It's sixty degrees today, though we've had a week of cold rain and frost in the suburbs.

William Bartram saw a green bittern on May 22 in the middle of a cold spring. Summers were bone dry some years, sultry with days in the nineties. In 1822 his notation for July 15 and the days that followed was "the garden, want rain in."

July was cool and wet in 1802: "Evening serene & cool wind notherly . . . wet harvest grain grows in the Ricks in the Harvest field." He wrote that it was "cool enough to sit comfortably by the fire." That July there were "many cases of yellow fever in the City, said to be brot in a vessel from the Isle St. Domingo." The apples were ripe by the end of the month, and oats were harvested. In the garden *Lilium superbum* was in flower.

"We have a plant now in the Garden," he writes, "the stem of which is upwards of eleven feet high terminating in a pyramid at top composed of 32 perfect Flowers It exhibits a truly superb spectacle." He noted cicadas and whistling crickets and fireflies.

By August 1802 the Franklinia was in flower, and fever was increasing in the city. Not until December does he write that fever "ceased."

On a Monday and Tuesday in August 1806 he sold plants in Philadelphia on John Welche's wharf, on board a schooner.

Fall could be treacherous. One October he noted: "A tremendous stormy Night Trees Blown down, & vessels overset in the Delaware, many people drowned. This morning yet stormy wind N. & NW. Afternoon & evening the wind more moderate but cold."

There were northern lights in April in 1820, and on September 12 of that year he wrote: "Last night & this morning we were favoured, I may say blessed with copius showers of rain." By November he was having a hard time writing. A snowy winter followed, and in May he noted that the "wood robbin" had arrived and the plum, cherry, apple, pear, gooseberry flower. The sun was "red smoky" the day the blue linnet arrived and the turtle dove cooed.

Each day, like a prayer, William Bartram recorded the small life of the garden in a book no bigger than his palm. A shorthand for the miracle of bloom and feather.

# 26. Columbine

I'VE PLANTED A TINY GREEN COLUMBINE in the garden on the side of the house. It's perfectly shaped, and the bloom is lime colored with long bright yellow stamens. I bought it at a garden in the bend of the river across from where the shad spawn. The garden is in Gladwyne but Philadelphia is right across the river. It's a garden made over many years by Mary Gibson Henry, a woman inspired by William Bartram to collect native plants starting in the early part of the twentieth century. She carried the plants back from the swampy areas of the Gulf Coast or the high valleys of British Columbia and nestled them in the ground of her garden with just the right soil and conditions for them to survive in Pennsylvania on an old Quaker farm. Her granddaughters are in charge of the garden now, and each spring they have a plant sale.

I've been reading gardening books about small gardens. Our patio is very tiny here, and each book tells me I must have a focal point. Our garden has not come into focus yet, no strategic bit of garden ornament draws the eye. I'm drawn instead to individual plants. Sometimes I sneak out early in the morning and study the leaves and petals, snaky roots, and buds before anyone is coming by on the sidewalk.

All around us the trees are leafing out in their new green. On the river shad may be swimming upstream to spawn like they have for a million or so years. Two different sparrows hop on and off the deck. In the morning I hear their songs. The white-throated sparrow and the white-crowned sparrow. On their way through to somewhere else. The cardinal whistles, and the large woodpecker drinks sap from the pruned limbs of the elm. Peter Kalm wrote that the settlers complained about woodpeckers. The birds drilled holes in the apple trees.

Gladiolas knife their way out of the dirt and matted mulch. The ferns spread out in their tangy light green breadth. Everything is miniature and perfectly made.

Are all these enough for a miracle? Father Georges comes by on Saturday and admires the flowers in the bed along the side of the house. I don't discuss theology with him.

He tells me he rows. His father rowed and his uncle too. He grew up in Mt. Airy.

Our house sits at the intersection of our neighbors' paths. I watch Mary Robinson make her way to her job a block away, leaning on her cane as she walks past the window. She told us on Sunday that she used to play in the puddles of the ice house that stood near her house down the street. During Prohibition she would warn her father and his friends, playing cards and drinking in the ice house, that the police were coming around the corner.

She knows the shortcuts through the rectory to the church and lives in the house that her parents bought before she was born. In 1970, she told me the other day, she planted the tree in front of her house in honor of her son's return from Vietnam.

"It's too big now," she said. "I asked the city to cut it down, but they said I'm on a list."

When Scott carries bags of soil into the back patio, Mary Robinson walking by says: "My mother-in-law who lived in the house right next to mine used to go to the park and dig up soil there with the kids and I would say to her, 'You're teaching those kids to steal.' And she'd say, 'It's good stuff and it's free.'"

Sometimes I see Father Alberto as he strides down the street past our house on his way to the store. He straightens his shoulders and rushes ahead, dinner on his mind, his night to cook. Yann, an architect who looks like Mr. Clean, comes by in the morning on his way for coffee and later on his way to the gym. He's been up half the night drawing plans for new building projects. At two-thirty the children run past the garden, dressed in their uniforms of red and blue, all talk as they head for home. Some push themselves along the sidewalk on their shiny new scooters.

We see our neighbors in church or in Garden Fresh, the store on the corner, buying whole chickens. Once there was a fire on that corner, and the top two stories disappeared in the blaze. In the fall, pumpkins and little gourds stand in an orange row on bales of hay. More than a hundred years ago, just before our house was built, there were farms here, a high pleasant place up above the river climbing north into more hilly land.

I smell the chickens each morning roasting on a spit in the back of the store where five large men are cooking and chopping and wrapping.

Later in the day I know I'm a part of all this pleasant activity. Yann is deep in his office designing buildings, and all the other workers are ranged along Fairmount signing papers, or bundling flowers into a knot, or digging up old rutted pavement, or cooking today's special.

There is no silence here. Even the tiniest leaves seem to bristle with the air, bright, clear, and shining.

Yesterday Jose Gallardo came by to talk about sidewalks. He's repairing ours soon and he wanted to go over the squares that need to be replaced. He had originally counted eight, but now as we walk from one section of the sidewalk to the next he finds ten. At a hundred and fifty dollars a square that's a bit more.

"How old is this sidewalk?" I ask him and he shrugs, "Oh, about seventy-five years old."

"Wow."

"Yeah, they lasted a long time." He tells me that the sidewalk was made by a method no one uses anymore, too costly, too time-consuming. You spread a layer of cement and then roll small stones into the surface. After it's dry you spread a light layer of cement over that and then polish the surface. I examine the stones I'm about to lose, smooth and shiny like ocean rocks.

"Don't cut the tree roots," I say and he shrugs again. Round and short, he wears a plaid shirt buttoned halfway up over a T-shirt, a shadow of a beard on his round face, a shiny gold stud in his ear. Another pirate.

"Those trees are strong," he says. "You don't have to worry about the trees."

Soon the schoolchildren and my various neighbors will traverse the sidewalk around my house. Jose Gallardo wanted to spray orange marks on the squares of cement we agreed to replace.

"Don't do it," I said, "They may think more about the sidewalk then."

"Oh, and trip," he said.

"Yes," I said, knowing he was thinking about their welfare but I was thinking about lawsuits.

Is commitment a miracle? The columbine's persistence in shape and form, the silver maple I can see as I write, exuberantly green, Mary Robinson growing up and marrying and living her long life all in the same house on the same street in the same city.

Last week I went on a field trip with my son and his class. We traveled to the edge of town along the river in a yellow bus. The bus went north and then east on the high flat hill where wealthy men built their large houses in the eighteenth and nineteenth centuries. Once we left the river we drove past gray and brown buildings on the black and gray pavement until we came to the art school. I was surprised by green, spilling all around me as I stepped from the bus to the grass. We were on the edge of Philadelphia. It was an old estate. We walked quickly to a barn where two young men and a young woman showed us how to blow glass into shapes. This too seemed to be a kind of miracle. The elements of the glass heated into liquid and then blown and pulled and heated and cooled into a shape completely artificial and breakable.

I admired the tools. "They're from Italy," Graham's art teacher told me. The narrow tongs and wide spatula, the wooden cradles of the glass balloons, the bucket of water, the glory hole of the burning stove.

Today is the Ascension. Christ risen from the dead and walking once again with his disciples disappears into the clouds. Except, Graham learns, we partake of his body and blood at communion in the Mass.

"It's not really like that," he said to me yesterday. "Is it? It's a little ghoulish if it is."

He's reading a book called *Grossology* but this idea of eating somebody's body is too much. "It's cannibalism," he said.

"It's not really," I say. "If you want, just think of it as a symbol." I notice that his catechism book is vague on the whole body and blood aspect too.

He's making his first communion this weekend in Our Lady of the Snows church, where he was baptized, far away from here in Vermont. My husband and I were married almost ten years ago in this same church and my father's burial Mass took place there, too.

Now the school bell is ringing and a truck clatters down the street. I'm poised above my tiny yard, typing in a room that looks out on the school and the street and the children in their red and blue uniforms filing into the building from the schoolyard. This schoolyard is just a parking lot and a concrete staircase. It reminds me of where I played when I was in second grade. The schoolyard was behind a Catholic school that looked a lot like St. Francis Xavier School. A picture of my large class from that year shows a smiling small girl sitting at a tiny desk in a roomful of students all dressed in the same kind of uniform that the students at the end of the street wear. The pleated skirt, the little white blouse.

The students are bent over their desks, moving their pencils in their workbooks, watching as the teacher writes and writes on the board. How secure they are for just that moment, their task at hand, their heads bent to it, all the weather outside them now as they copy a word onto the bright new page.

# 27. Morning Glory

I MUST MAKE A CONFESSION. I now have a focal point, or at least the garden does. I realized this not long ago as I stood in the center of the patio and looked at the bamboo. It's feathery and lovely, bending its long canes this way and that in the dry May wind we've been having now for several weeks. Transplanted, exotic and content in its two pots.

"Is it a drought yet?" I asked my husband this morning.

"Not officially," he said.

William Bartram's garden suffered in this same kind of heat almost two hundred years ago. The soil is like dust.

The samara of the elm are dry but potent sprouting in all the pots I've placed in the garden and on the deck. In the community garden the seeds of all the flowers I planted are slow to germinate in the dry heat.

Sometimes things just don't take root and thrive. Sometimes gardeners overwater them or coddle them with fertilizer when all they need is time.

Down the street from us the rubble and trash along the narrow alley by a house is covered by morning glories, bright blue flowers popping out over tires and plastic wrappers and pieces of wood. Someone has swept behind a motorcycle that's stood unused for a year. There's a great abundance here. Abundance of heat, of food, of trash, of water, of river, of bird (the hawks hunting in the park, the pigeons lining the street, the cardinal singing in the elm in the morning), of age, of loss, of word, of hair, of bread.

We're all a bit of home, homeless, homebound in this homeland.

Attached in our own ways to a pot of bamboo or a brick house or a slip of a house that was once a shell on the edge of a sewer that was once a stream in the meadows along the river that once meandered to the sea.

The grass is brown along the Parkway and clipped dry in the baseball field as I circle once and then again, running hard on white clover and spiky grass, past a row of sycamores and along the dark poplars, running hard on the sloping fields that were once Springettsbury.

Near the new children's climber in the park two, or perhaps three, men are camping out. As I run past I try to figure out if the bundle of black plastic bags and clothes in the little fruit tree is a sleeping person or just someone's possessions. Another man is sorting his wet clothes on two benches and sloshing water in a plastic paint bucket. It smells like disinfectant as I pass going in the opposite direction, counterclockwise.

Sometimes one or two of the men in the park will come down Wallace Street on garbage morning inspecting my neighbor's bags and boxes of garbage. Once someone dumped the leaves I had shoveled into a bag on the sidewalk into a neat pile and stole the plastic bag.

"He was washing the sidewalk," Scott tells me when he comes back from his walk. "That guy in the park was washing the sidewalk."

"Oh that's what the disinfectant smell was," I reply. "How was he washing it?"

"Very carefully with a mop."

## 28. *Mint*

A MAP OF PHILADELPHIA published in 1796 shows Springetts-bury and nearby Bush Hill, a house built on land purchased from William Penn. Our community garden—The Spring Gardens—sits at the top of the slope above Bush Hill beyond a grove of evergreens that grows in an ordered grid north of the house. It's a cultivated block in the place where the little stream flowed through down to woodland and formal garden below. Now the stream has disappeared, fed underground in one of the sewer pipes, but I see it sometimes on the baseball field, bubbling up in the indentations near the Parkway.

Abigail Adams stayed in Bush Hill and wrote a letter to her sister in 1791 after a long winter when they "consumed forty cords of wood in four months."

"A very beautiful place" where sheep pastured on the lawn in front of the house.

She writes, "I am told that this spot is very delightful as a summer residence. The house is spacious. The views from it are rather beautiful than sublime; the country round has too much of the level to be in my style. The appearance of uniformity wearies the eye, and confines the imagination. We have a fine view of the whole city from our windows; a beautiful grove behind the house, through which there is a spacious gravel walk, guarded by a number of marble statues, whose genealogy I have not yet studied, as the last week is the first time I have visited them."

Graham and I met Manuel in the community garden this morning. I was filling my green plastic bucket at the large blue container someone had filled to the brim with water. He asked, "Habla usted español?" and I shook my head and said no.

"I just moved here," he said, "over on Spring Garden. Do you like to garden?"

I nodded yes and smiled, shifting the watering can in my hand.

"I sold my big house in the Northeast and moved to the Caribbean and now I'm back. I didn't like it there, no health insurance, and the doctors aren't good. I had a block, bought it in 1980 for thirty-five thousand dollars. I planted that whole block. I still have forty acres in the Dominican Republic, hired seventeen men to grow tobacco. I grow everything. What are you planting?"

"Flowers," I answer. "Too early for tomatoes."

"No," he says. "You cover them with a plastic milk jug—and I tell you, pour Miracle-Gro around a circle around the edges and they'll grow very big."

It's been a dry spring, and each day I walk to the garden to try to coax the flower seeds into sprouting. Yesterday Graham and I watered the tiny rows of zinnias and cosmos and coreopsis and dill, mostly hidden in their sheaths of hard seed under the silty soil, dry now for almost a month.

On our way to the garden we pass two older women who sit on their adjoining stoops talking. Sometimes one of the women is carrying handfuls of lettuce or beans back from the garden. Down the street a bit farther, a bent woman with long white hair sweeps the sidewalk back and forth with a little broom. Often men sit on a bench across from the garden smoking and drinking beer. Sometimes I see an older man with a straw hat and a younger man with dark hair touring the gardens pointing to this or that, conversing in Spanish. When I say hello to them, they nod.

Last fall I shoveled slim elm leaves we gathered from the trees near our house into the dark soil of our square patch of ground. Not long ago, ten years perhaps, this neighborhood was strewn with several blocks of rotting buildings. People dumped water heaters and garbage, old tires and washing machines where I now turn the soil. One of our neighbors told us that his father used to dump old toilets and refrigerators in the empty lots that bordered the crack houses.

"You never knew what you'd find there," he said.

The park near the garden was filled with drug dealers. Everyone knew who they were. And then the city pulled the houses down.

On the way back from the garden I saw a woman carry an armful of large leeks into her house. The windows are boarded up on the first floor, but sometimes she puts her house plants on a ledge on the second floor. She exposes them to weather above the street. She carried the leeks like a child in her arms, the long gray-green tops flopping off to the side.

"Onions," said Graham.

"No, leeks," I said, and we continued down the street. Earlier I carried my own bundle of daylilies from the boathouses near the art museum, the lilies' knotty little tubers pressed against my shirt. I saved them from the dumpster. I walked past the waterworks and up the hill and placed them on the dry sidewalk near my garden, arms spattered with dirt.

There's a lot to gather up here. The weather forecast tells me it might rain today. A man I met on Friday told me that rainwater is much better than city water.

"Less chemicals," his friend told me. She was cleaning my husband's classroom while Graham and I waited for Scott.

"I think I'll put out a can and catch me some rainwater," she said. "My mother used to do that to water the houseplants, much better for them."

She's from South Carolina. "When I retire," she told me, "I'm going back there. I thought it was so strange when I moved here, the houses all connected and no grass. I want to have a yard. I miss a nice green yard."

She told me she likes vacuuming, it reminds her of cutting the lawn. It's relaxing.

The man told me he grows sixty bushels of sweet potatoes near Grays Ferry up the river from Bartram's Garden on railroad land.

"They're sweet when they're little," he says. "We used to go into the field and eat them raw, little ones as big as my thumb. I just put the baskets of potatoes out on my porch and my neighbors know they can take them."

Our first summer here Graham planted zinnias and pumpkins, zucchini and bachelor buttons, and I threw in some wildflowers and garlic chives in our plot in the community garden. We planted quickly, too quickly. We were horrified when we saw how fast and large everything grew. Our neighbors wanted to hack away at our wandering pumpkin and looked on with pleasure when we finally snipped the monster vines back.

Things grow well here.

We harvested our pumpkin early in the fall, a large perfect globe of bright orange, smooth and sweet to smell if you put your nose close to the skin. It was hidden under the sunflowers, snuggled up near the rough stalk of one of the giants. We were afraid one of the local thieves would steal the pumpkin if we left it in the garden too long.

One of my neighbors in the garden, who talks to his friend as he runs his hand over his peppers or hoes between his rows of beans, plants cilantro in the fall. The lacy light green leaves are two inches high in November. He harvests his beans, peppers, and tomatoes all summer and plants several corn stalks on the corners of his garden.

I've seen other gardens like ours around the city. One day on the train we sped by a huge expanse of garden in North Philadelphia called Glenwood Green Acres. Gardeners who moved north from farms in the South during the 1960s grow sweet potatoes, cotton, and peanuts. In Chinatown gardens are tucked into squares between parking lots, with big white plastic buckets at the corners of green rows of vegetables.

Sometimes you can go to the garden and no one is there at all. A rose tree with polished buds about to bloom looks like the Alice in Wonderland roses, a peony bush as large as a cupboard, a red trumpet vine festooned on a spindly fence, lambs ears growing up into their boring blooms, a robin daring to pick a leaf of lettuce in my neighbor's garden, a pale spider transplanted on a shovel of new wood chips to the sandy bed of my plot.

"I was a builder, I built a big house on that block," Manuel says later as I'm digging in my garden, turning the soil over with a red-handled trowel. "You going to pull up all that mint?"

"Have some," I say, and he takes my trowel and digs fistfuls.

"I'll put it in the front of the house, you got anything to put it in?" I hand him a plastic bag.

"I'll take a little soil," he says. "It's always good to take some of the soil it's growing in—grows better."

A large bumblebee is lumbering by my nose. I'm on my knees flipping the warm earth over, patting soil over the red and yellow kernels of ornamental corn.

The gardeners in the community garden cultivate the same vegetables the Romans brought to the countries they occupied and cultivated. We're not so different, planting our cauliflower and onions and peas and beans after the early spinach and garden cress, parsley and lettuces. If Abigail Adams had had a garden at Bush Hill, she would have cultivated the same kinds of vegetables, but they would have fancy names like Rounceval and Hotspur peas. She would have to let the best plants go to seed and collect and save the seed for the following season, or order the seeds from England, or travel the muddy four miles to the wharf in Philadelphia to buy from the sea captains who sold garden seeds on the dock.

The swift erasing of time is working on me as I lean against the dirt, but I can disregard my stiff hands for at least a few hours. My son is running in the wild part of the garden. Look, he's throwing the severed bamboo stalk like a javelin. Soon he'll retrieve it from the path and start all over again.

## 29. Sunflower

I'M DIPPING THE RED PLASTIC BUCKET into a large blue container of water. As I pull the bucket up filled to the brim with clear lukewarm water I slosh a bit on my hands. Did Ann Bartram have a well where she drew her water those early years on her farm? I can't remember. Or did the Bartrams draw water from the river? I know there was a well later. John Bartram mentions it in his will.

Goldfinches hang from a cluster of purple sunflowers near me, and when I carry the bucket down the path to my plot in the community garden, I brush against the rough, sharp stalks of an ornamental grass grown to eight feet in my neighbor's a garden. It's almost a hundred degrees, and the air sucks the water from the earth immediately. I dump ten or more buckets on the tiny roots of cosmos and coreopsis, miniature Indian corn and peony, a boxwood bush I've rescued from the adoption plot, and the tall bent figures of the sunflowers my son loves.

A tall man dressed in black yells from the sidewalk, "You know where the owner is?"

"No, I don't," I yell back.

Now I'm talking to George, who's stopped by to take a look at things. I hand him my clippers and say, here cut yourself some flowers.

The tall man comes through the new fence and says, "An Italian man that lives over there wants to rent a plot."

"It's Steve," I say, "who does that."

"Oh yeah, I know, I told him that."

"He's not the owner, he just signs people up." I can see how he might think Steve owns the place. Steve is an architect who strides around much of the time in a kind of African bush outfit directing gangs of men as they pave the sidewalks or position the fence. But he's doing it all for free, I think.

The tall man disappears and then comes back. "Got a bag?" he asks. I pull a plastic bag from under a pile of weeds I've set aside for the compost heap.

"I found this one," I say. And I hold it as he plops his large ripe tomatoes into the wet interior.

"Sure you don't want some?"

"No, I've got tomatoes on my deck."

"I grow melons on my windowsill, little ones, like this," he says, and holds his large hands in a cup.

"That's a fig tree," George says and points to a low, leafy tree in the middle of a neighbor's plot. "You can eat them ripe off the tree."

We've been examining water these hot days. No water to swim in near us unless we plunged into the Schuylkill with the geese and ducks and skinny heron. A few days ago we followed the river to Hawk Mountain, where in the fall raptors fly quite close to the ledge that points north. In the late nineteenth century and early twentieth, hundreds of men would stand on the long ridge and kill thousands of migrating birds as they flew close to the rocky edge.

John Bartram took the same trip on his way to Onondaga, the council seat of the Six Nations, in New York in 1743. It was a hot day in early July. He followed the river north and west past Indian towns like Shamokin and the house of one of his companions, a negotiator named Conrad Weiser, who called himself "an ambassador to the Indians." Bartram's first version of the narrative of this journey was lost in 1744 on its way to Peter Collinson in England, when the ship that carried the manuscript was captured by the French. Two other copies of the work disappeared. The book was finally published in England in 1751: "made publick without the author's knowledge."

Bartram swam in rivers "so clear one might have seen a pin at the bottom" and hung up his "blanket like a hammock." He passed old Indian fields with "excellent soil" surrounded by the footsteps of deserted towns—peach trees, plums and "excellent grapes." He was accompanied by Weiser, who spoke Iroquois, cartographer Lewis Evans from Philadelphia, and Shickellamy, a man they met in Shamokin, "the chief man in the town, which consisted of Delaware Indians." Shickellamy was an Oneida chief and the Six Nations ambassador to Pennsylvania. His son went along too, to settle an affair with the Iroquois at Onondaga. Two Shawnee warriors had been killed in the backcountry of Virginia.

They followed the branches of the Susquehanna through "a vale of pine land" and then traveled past a place where Bartram saw signs of an Indian ceremony:

> They cut a parcel of poles, which they stick in the ground in a circle, about the bigness of hop poles, the circle about five foot diameter, and then bring them together at the top, and tie them in the form of an oven, where the conjurer placeth himself. Then his assistants cover the cage over close with blankets and to make it still more suffocating, hot stones are rolled in. After all this the priest must cry aloud and agitate his body . . . before the stubborn spirit will become visible to him, which they say is generally in the shape of a bird. There is usually a stake drove into the ground about four foot high and painted. I suppose this they design for the winged airy Being to perch upon, while he reveals to the invocant what he has taken so much pains to know.

Their route took them through great forests of oak, chestnut, white pine, poplar, and white oak. One grove of white pine was "so very lofty & so close that the sun could hardly shine through."

We drove when Bartram and his companions would have walked or ridden horses through the dense woods along the river, winding and folding and curving back on itself as we gained altitude from the flat of the coastal plain. Indian trails were only twelve to eighteen inches wide and covered with briars and blocked by fallen trees.

Now the banks were very green, resplendent in the heat, all shimmer of leaf and water. Near the origin of the Schuylkill it split into two main tributaries, and the creek was flat and wide and shallow, filled with silt from a recent thunderstorm.

We were in a country of large farms, the fields spread in rectangles on the sides of sloping hills, the dark tall trees come down to the creek from old woodlots or other overgrown fields. There were yellow stone houses and large barns with decorated boards. Some of the farms would have been here when Bartram was traveling through. Perhaps he stopped at one or another for dinner and a place to sleep before journeying farther north and west away from the settlements.

John Bartram was traveling north for botanical as well as political reasons. By that time his friendship and business arrangement with Peter Collinson had been going on for almost ten years. Bartram's boxes of a hundred envelopes of various seeds had been sent through Collinson to patrons like Lord Petre, who had a very large collection of American trees and shrubs, and also to nurserymen and more ordinary people. Each box cost five guineas—a month's wages. If Bartram's customers were lucky and coaxed the seeds into sprouting in a hotbed, after a year they might have the very beginning of a *Magnolia grandiflora*, with its shiny green leaves and white waxy blossoms, or a witch hazel blooming in winter, or a pink azalea. Gardeners planted the American trees in a little wilderness or in clusters for sylvan walks. Eventually they were placed in a shrubbery, where ladies could wander safely. The trees were admired for their yellow leaves in the fall, or their flowers, or the color of their needles, or the shape of their stems against the light.

One of Bartram's biographers, Thomas Slaughter, writes that Bartram collected about one fourth of all the North American plants identified and sent to Europe during the colonial period. He was called the greatest botanist of his day by Linnaeus.

Thomas Penn had chosen him for this trip to explore the country beyond Philadelphia. Bartram noted that the woods were thick with ginseng, and he could hear the musical howling of the wolf.

"Now I know," I said when we got home, "where the river comes from and where it goes. Now I know what color the water is before it comes here and how it twists and turns and folds back on itself."

"I should hope so," Scott said. "It was a really long drive."

"Yeah," said Graham. "And it was hot too."

The sunflowers love this water from the river, soaking it up in their twisted white roots. Their heads bend above me as I empty the bucket.

# 30. *Poinsettia*

DURING A HOT JULY IN 1830 a committee of gardeners from the Pennsylvania Horticultural Society tromped from garden to garden in the "vicinity" of Philadelphia. In their report published the following February they note that it was too hot to see everything. They left out the vegetable gardens "where Leguminous plants of every kind are so copiously and so successfully cultivated." I think it was a paradise of sorts here then, even in the sweltering heat of July.

Mr. Breck had a garden on the Schuylkill across the river from Lemon Hill on the west bank. His greenhouse was full of lemon, orange, and citron trees in "fine bearing." He had an English oak raised from an acorn and a hedge of white hawthorn planted in 1810 "plashed, stalked, and dressed last Spring by two Englishmen, who understood the business well."

Not too far out of town Mr. Smith grew a banana tree (*Musa* × *paradisiaca*) "in fine flower." It was ten feet tall and planted in a greenhouse that Mr. Smith expected to heat in the winter with a steam engine.

Mr. Hibbert grew two thousand camellias on a lot packed with "green and hot houses" on Chestnut Street. And D. and C. Landreth grew magnolias not far from there in their gardens. In the spring the nurserymen grew fifty different kinds of double hyacinths.

Lemon Hill was kept "in perfect order at a great expense." It was, the committee wrote, "the best kept garden in Pennsylvania . . . unrivalled in the Union." Sweet bushes vanished now were covered with straw in the winter—thunbergias, mimosas, tree sage, and South Sea tea.

Mr. Pratt's green houses were "220 feet long by 16 broad; exhibiting the finest range of glass for the preservation of plants, on this continent." His ponds held fish. I know the committee stood on the hill under the searing heat of that July day and admired the cool flash of the silver fish, the glinting gold. I know the pool was cool somehow even in the heat of July.

When the committee visited Bartram Botanic Garden and Nursery, William Bartram's niece Nancy and her husband, Robert Carr, ran the business. William had died in the garden seven years before in another hot July. Eighty-four, he had spent the morning writing at his desk that looked out at the river. He had given away all his possessions except two chests of clothes, a feather bed and bolster, two glasses and a tray, a tin letter box, some books, and a purse with cash. He lived most of the last half of his life in his garden.

The garden, the committee reported, "was established as early as 1720, by that great vegetable naturalist John Bartram the elder, at a time when nothing of the kind existed in the then Colonies, except Dr. Clayton's in Virginia." The collection, they note, is 110 years old and contains "many of the indigenous plants and trees of North America." More than two thousand native species were planted in the six acres.

Robert Carr is listed as the proprietor of the garden, but Ann Carr, or "Nancy," was the expert behind the business. Trained by her uncle, William, and her father, John, she was a skilled artist and botanist. She was five when her mother died, and she lived in the house at Bartram's garden with her grandmother Ann and famous uncle and her father and a sister and two brothers. She might have been in love with Alexander Wilson, a poet and teacher from Scotland who wrote and illustrated the first book on American birds. She married his printer, though, in March 1809.

I saw a print not long ago cut from one of the volumes of Wilson's work. Nancy may have colored the plate for the print. I imagine her bent over, hard at work, as Robert Carr opened the door to his shop. Her wedding gown still hangs from a wooden peg in her house, a small dress of shimmering green and gold silk.

In 1819 the Carrs were struggling to make the garden profitable. Robert Carr wrote, "The advanced age of our uncle, Mr. W. B., who resides with us and who could not bear the thought of parting with the garden, forbids the idea of selling during his life." By 1830 the garden was flourishing. Carr employed twenty men and boys, he wrote, "nearly all year." In June 1829 the Carrs exhibited the first cultivated poinsettia in Philadelphia.

Twenty years later they were forced to sell the property to a wealthy man who built a brick-turreted mansion on one of the fields that sloped to the river.

On that hot day in July of 1830 the committee members were impressed with the "minutest Marchantia" and the "loftiest Cypress." There was an eighty-foot-tall magnolia tree and a Kentucky coffee tree in bloom. They toured the vineyard where Robert and Nancy grew 145 kinds of grapes by the river. There were 800 camellias and a sago palm in one of the greenhouses and a lemon tree grown from seed. A *Testudinaria elephantipes* was 150 years old.

The large fruit orchard was filled with trees—113 varieties of apples, 72 pears, 39 peaches, and several other sweet fruits. They grew 30 different kinds of honeysuckle.

The garden must have been heavy with the scent on that hot day of fruiting trees and ripe flowers and the bent stems of the flowering honeysuckle. John Bartram's pond was filled with gold and silver fish. The shining fish were for sale, like all the other fruits of the garden. If you went to the garden now you could put your hand on the indentation in the middle of the lower garden that was once the pond. Soil samples show where the silky water once reflected the limbs of a very old baldcypress. The clay soil of the eighteenth-century pond is still wet under the fill of the 1930s. A stream flowed down the garden to the river, and the cool, shallow, green river flowed past on its way to the cold ocean.

In 1767 William Bartram drew a picture of the plants growing at the lip of the pond: the spiky mouth of a Venus flytrap or the "Tipiti-witchet Sensitive" coveted by Peter Collinson and first cultivated by John Bartram in 1762, and the huge leaves of colocasia or American lotus, *Nelumbo lutea*, some of the flowers held upright in a tight bud, others completely open. A heron, tiny under a colocasia leaf, bends his neck toward the water. Attentive, he spears one of the gold or silver fish with his beak. The seeds, John Bartram wrote to Collinson in 1768, "came up the second spring after sowing."

He sent roots of the colocasia to the King in a barrel with two bull-frogs who loved to "sit to air themselves under other broad leaves that riseth two foot above like A canopy but here thay seldom roar."

If you sailed or rowed upriver in the 1860s, the wet banks by Bartram's garden and along the river for "nearly two miles" would be full of the American lotus, the wide leaves, and the waxy petals of the flower.

# 31. Rose

I WANT TO BE CHARMED BY THE CITY but I'm not. Not by the woman with the perky little dog who greets me on her travels, not by the man sleeping in the park as I run several times past, his encampment a brown sheet, a brown paper bag, a shopping cart with a symbolic fan that's real, propped on its side, a few possessions near his head, boots, a shirt—by the third time around the baseball fields he's stretching, one arm held up to the sun. Not by the cluster of birds in the dead fruit tree, starlings and sparrows and crows, companions in the morning that's heating up with each circle around the fields. Not by the man rousing himself on a bench or the other adjusting his shoes near his feet, not by the handmade table propped by the Sisters behind their convent on two stumps, not by the single rose blooming in their garden. Not by the falling leaves of the sycamores, crumpling in the dry heat, not by the fountain spewing silver water, not by the little boy learning to walk right in front of our door, not by the blue jay calling in the morning or the fat spider strung up on the clematis and tomato on the deck. Not by two matching children with backpacks, both miniatures of their tall mother or the church smelling cool as I walk past up the street. Not by the word "lucky" scrawled in a sidewalk, not by putting one foot and then another into the letters as I walk.

# 32. Gingko

I AM HOEING. Leaning into the pull and tug of the flat, sharp hoe against the dry soil. Dry, I discover, only an inch or two on the top. The depths are cool even in this heat. Yesterday I was looking for Ann Bartram again. I went to Bartram's Garden and read for a couple of hours in the attic above her dairy where the archives are now kept. It was cool and quiet there. I shared the room with three students who were working on the archeological dig around the main house. They were fiddling on computers this morning, making outlines of blue rooms on their machines.

"She must have been an amazing woman to have such an amazing son. You would think she had some influence on him," Joel Fry, the archivist, said as he handed me two folders.

I read John Bartram's will, where he made sure to provide for his wife's comfort:

> I gaive and bequeath to my son John Bartram all my plantation
> whereon we live scituate between David Gibsons land and my son
> James Bartrams land with all the apurtenances to it both upland and
> medow to him and his heairs forever he paying his mother yearly ten
> pounds, and is to find her sufficient firewood cut and hauled to the
> dore of her kitchen and keep her a cow and horse winter and summer
> on good grass or hay and allso a sufficient spot in his garden to sow
> or plant on, and full liberty to pass and repass to the well and rooms
> here mentioned that is the new seller and the two rooms above it and
> the parlor and chamber over it and the ould stoveroom now used for
> a kitshen all which she must claim during her natural life as her full
> right according to my will.

"We know she went into Philadelphia to sell a pitcher plant. But we don't know how she got there," a volunteer told me. Did she take a ferry, did she sell her butter and eggs when she got there?

"She must have had a wagon," I said.

And she said, "Yes, but we don't know about any of that, you see she was a woman. This family didn't save letters, it was only John's they eventually saved. Most were sold when they ran into money problems."

When John Bartram died in September 1777, the inventory of his house included in the Small Room: "One Twenty four Hour Clock, 1 Old Desk, One Old Tea Table, 1 Small Close Iron Stove & Funell, A Feather Bed, Bolster & 2 Pillows, 7 pr. Sheets, Bolster & Pillow Cases, 1 Cover Lid & 1 pr. Blankets Old, 1 Bed Stead, 9 Rush Bottom Chairs, 2 Old Fire Shovels & 1 pr. Tongs, & 1 Hand Brush." The Large Chamber had a table and a bed and "One Looking Glass with Sconces, Pewter Dishes & Plates, One Spining Whel, 2 Brass candlesticks & 2 Iron, One Delf Bowl & Dish, A Small Floore Cloth," and a few other items. An Upper Room contained a looking glass, another bed and quilt, three stone plates, and two leather-bottom chairs. In the Back Room was another bed and blankets, "One Chest, 1 Set of Globes (Broke), Library of Books."

I am hoeing in the heat climbing up to ninety today, but yesterday I stood under the trees that John Bartram planted three hundred years ago. The air was cool. The river ran the opposite way, backing itself away from the sea, high tide, and chocolate colored from the big rains we had a few days before.

I stood under the largest ginkgo tree in America, a gift from a wealthy man who had an estate just up the river from John Bartram's house and farm and garden.

A few days ago I went to a gathering of poets. We were all women, sipping our wine and eating the delicious food two other poets had prepared. Our host's backyard was once part of a large extended yard where fruit trees and gardens grew for the houses on that block, built in the 1830s. She shares a very old ginkgo with her neighbors. It towers above her small yard and its thorny orange trees and little lights in tiny pagodas. She showed me where a yellow-bellied sapsucker drills holes each year. The ginkgo trunk is full of the marks of the sapsucker. I was very happy thinking of all these things, the bird and the tree and the gathering of women who had already made sure that what they said and thought and felt would be recorded.

Once we met a man gathering ginkgo berries on the sidewalk near the art museum in late fall. I asked him what he did with them.

"We eat them," he said, "for dessert." He was scraping the stinky berries into a pile on the sidewalk with a drywall knife.

Ginkgoes grow in northern China. He's from the south—so it's paradise, he told me, to have as many as he wants.

"We think it's amazing that people are walking on them here."

It's the same climate in Philadelphia as northeast China, he tells me. The ginkgo leaf is slightly poisonous, like the berries, and is used for medicines. He puts the berries, slipped from their shells, in a white plastic mixing bucket—piled one against the other in their shiny skins.

"We make a pudding of the berries," he says.

Yesterday I stood at the edge of the meadow at Bartram's garden on the border of the property, originally part of their farm and later lost to development along the river. Now slender swallows dip and swirl above the long grasses. I could see our bend in the river as I looked north. I could see the green border of river and the trees that came down from Fairmount. I thought about the richness of ginkgoes in the city, the spare inventory of items in John Bartram's house, the place in the garden reserved for Ann.

# Gladwyne

GREAT EXOTIC BUTTERFLIES,

SNOW-WHITE AND

MARVELOUSLY FRAGRANT

# 33. Auricula

MY FATHER IS BURIED IN A PASTURE. Across the road from the pasture is the cold stone crypt where they used to keep the bodies in the winter until the ground thawed enough for burial in the spring. His pasture is at the top of a hill that looks out over the rolling pastures below and wood lots and the little streams flowing into the Brownsville Brook. The mountain he loved, Ascutney, is a blue triangle against the milky sky. Stone walls line the perimeter of the graveyard. Farmers built them in moonlight, too busy to clear the fields during the day. I suppose this is a garden of sorts, the kind of landscape that's been called into creation by its usefulness. Cows and horses once pastured here. An old orchard provides deer with frozen apples and pears in the winter, a farmer still grows corn on that patch to the right, and, until Mrs. Hilt's death, horses cropped the sweet cold grass on the other side of the wall.

The room where I write in the tall narrow house was once bordered by pastures too. Large farms on rolling land going north, wedged between the wide Delaware and the smaller rush of the Schuylkill.

The Quaker farms that surrounded me were admired by their owners for their usefulness. They could provide their families with fruits and vegetables, pasture for sheep and horses, milk from the cow, herbs for medicine, even citrus for the winter months from trees wintered in greenhouses. Sometimes they sent their produce to Philadelphia, to sons and daughters with small yards behind narrow houses.

Isaac Norris built a country house in 1712–17 not far from William Penn's land at Springettsbury, northeast toward the Delaware River. A successful merchant, friend and executor of William Penn, he had a house in Philadelphia but eventually sold it and moved to

Fairhill. Not long after he bought the land for his plantation and built his house, he wrote to a friend in England, "We are now moved a great way from the temperate climate & delightful isle. Instead of the beautiful prospects of enclosure & gay improvements we are surrounded with woods & all nature in its rough dress."

His place was a working farm with several buildings. By 1726 he had a stable, a brew house, a barn, springhouse, wash house, stone kitchen, granary, corn house, cider house, milk house, smokehouse, shop shed, greenhouse—one of the earliest in Philadelphia—and a "garden closet," a room connected to the greenhouse, "an inner chamber." He added a cow house, barrack, hen house, brick kiln, coach house, boat house, and coach stable. He was able to provide his large family with food, fuel, and clothing from his farm. His daughter Deborah writes to her brother Isaac Jr., an apprentice in England, in 1733: "We bake our own bread but brew not our own beer, because thou sold all our molasses, & stock's low, and make our candles . . . Father has promised all the wood we burn this winter. I value myself that I can so readily conform to a change. I think I promise fair for frugality, but whether I shall perform in all I'll not say."

Some of the details of the Norris family's life at Fairhill are noted in tiny script in almanacs at the Library Company, a library founded by Benjamin Franklin. I looked at the small books about the size of my hand. They were leather and worn. The librarian brought me several from the years 1713 to 1738. Isaac Norris had written his name on the first page of each almanac. Two were his son's, dated after Isaac's death in 1735.

He wrote in 1713 that he was beginning to plant the orchard. Eventually, it contained espaliered and standard fruit trees bordered by a stone wall. He grafted his own varieties and ordered twelve different kinds of pear trees, seven cherry, nine apricot, and nine plum from an English nursery. One year he planted "Indian Corne" in the "Young Orchard." By 1720 he had "sett quick privatt hedge al along front of young orchard."

In the fall he sold livestock and had seventy-five sheep and forty-four lambs. He kept track of how much money he got for each part of an animal he slaughtered—the meat, the tallow, and the "hyde." Norris planted wheat, oats, Indian corn, rye, winter barely, turnips, and tobacco. His lists include the dates of when he started haying in June and where the hay was cut: new Barn field, long meadow, new meadow, behind old barn, cow pen, wet steep back meadow. In 1731 July was exceedingly hot and in August, "rain and cool."

Like John Bartram, he experimented with crop rotation and harvested wheat. He sold sixty apple trees to his friend James Logan.

His kitchen garden was planted with carrots, radish, cabbage, lettuce, celery, savoy, endive, cauliflower, spinach, English beans from Thomas Penn, Rounceval peas, gray peas, red peas, and Bermuda potatoes. One year he planted five beds of asparagus.

His family was supplied with honey from his several hives: a straw hive, garden hive, a middle colony, and a hollow tree hive on a low stool in the bee shelter. In 1730 in May he noted "we had 2 swarms of Bees com out."

The bees could dine on wildflowers or his cultivated mixture of poppies, double larkspur, wallflowers, Persian iris, daffodils, pinks, and tulips in what might have been a formal design.

In the greenhouse, a long building with glass on the south side, he wintered citrus trees, moving them outside when the weather warmed. October could be cold—on the fifteenth in 1725 there was "small hail" and it was "very cold on this night" with "frost the first Black frost."

I can imagine what the farm smelled like. I once worked on a farm in northern Norway. Each kind of grass had its own smell, the wet matted grass by the river, the long dry grass on the hills. The warm breath of the cows in the barn and the acrid smell of the manure I shoveled out of the stalls. The sharp, hot smell of haying. And the cool damp night as I walked a graveled path to the dairy to scoop up the milk in a white pitcher.

At Fairhill there was a long gravel walk that led past an orchard to the front door. In many of the "ephemeris," or almanacs, there were lists of projects for the year. In 1720 Norris wanted to "gravel & levell the backyard" and gravel the walks to the kitchen garden. A gate with stout finials on the curved tips of the wood opened to the inner courtyard, where one large tree stood. One of his rooms was painted blue, and the cupola on the top of the turret had a "weather-cock" and a compass at the base to show the wind direction.

The bricks for his house were made from clay dug on the hill and some of the boards were made from timber he sawed from his woods. Like many Quakers in Philadelphia, he owned slaves, William and Addoo, and they helped make the bricks and build the house. They also worked for other farmers who needed help with haying or brick-work.

A drawing from the mid-eighteenth century shows an ordered landscape with lines of fruit trees and rectangles of fences sur-rounding pasture, garden, house, barn, and other small buildings. The weathercock is very large on the top of the turret. Everything is symmetrical and ordered.

Not far from Fairhill is Stenton, James Logan's house. The sixty apple trees might have been planted quite close to the house he built on a sloping plot of land. Cattle grazed below the house and there was a stream that's gone now, sucked under the earth with all the small and large waters that once fed into the Delaware or the Schuylkill from the land that rises from the coastal plain.

Logan was Penn's secretary when he stepped off the ship *Canterbury* in 1699. His titles became more grand, and eventually he collected the most books of anyone in the colonies. He examined Indian corn trying to figure out how plants reproduced. Logan, like John Bartram, experimented with farming methods and cultivation. He had a large library and gave Bartram several books to read—*Bot-*

*anologia* by William Salmon and John Parkinson's herbal, more useful for identifying American plants. Logan and Bartram collaborated on dissecting flowers to examine the new system of classification that Carl Linnaeus invented in the 1730s.

His son William had a garden that Deborah Logan remembered having a greenhouse filled with "many rare and beautiful plants: indeed the large and fine orange and lemon trees which now ornament Pratt's greenhouses at Lemon Hill were originally of his raising . . . I know this to be so."

William's garden had bulbs and carnations, striped hollies, gold stripe rosemary, horseshoe-leaved geraniums, and yucca. Before his father's death he was ordering fruit trees and flowers from Elias Bland in England. An order written in 1749 requests six named varieties of cherries, plums, and carnations, "Let them stand upon the open deck. Take care the mise don't Eat them & keep them from stormy whether, you may lett them have gentell Rain but not too Mutch of itt nor too mutch Sun Shine don't lett the Salt Water wash them."

He added, "roots of tulips, Ranunculus, Narcissus, Dutch poppys, Seeds of double Larkspurs, Stocks of severall sorts, French & African marygolds, Sweet scented peas, with directions with them when to be sowed. Take care the mise don't eat them."

He sent for wild shrubs in 1753 from William Bodicker in Bucks County with these directions: "Send me down, carefully planted in two tubs, two or three handsome Bay trees or broad laurels. Let them be straight bodied, about 3 feet high at most, and about the thickness of one's thumb—not too large a head in proportion to its roots. They should come by water and be often wet by the boatmen." He wanted gooseberry bushes "of the wild sort" a year later and "some pretty flower roots."

In his directions to Thomas Bincks, another exporter of seeds and flowers, he gives a list and the method for transporting his plants:

> Flower roots to be sent—24 earliest Tulips sorted, 30 largest and very best hyacinths sorted, 50 double jonquils, 100 yellow and blue crocus that bloy in the fall of the year, 50 snow drops, 24 Persian Iris, 12 naked ladies, 20 double anemonies (if tuberose roots are plenty and cheap send me some of them also), 8 pots of carnations, 8 pots of auriculas (Let them be Good and the Potts be put into a course Rough Box made with a shelving lid so as it may throw the water at sea when the weather is bad and yet be half open when good so as the Sun may not come too Violently on the Auricula plants.)

Auricula, or bear's ear or primrose. The striped or rimmed petal dusted with a "farina" that washed away in heavy rains. Found wild in the Alps, the auricula was cultivated starting in the late sixteenth century in England.

Mark Laird writes in *The Flowering of the English Landscape Garden* that in 1691 Mary, first Duchess of Beaufort, had over one hundred auriculas in pots, beds, and borders. William Logan may have read about auricula cultivation in Philip Miller's *The Gardeners Dictionary*, or perhaps he witnessed their cultivation in England. Perhaps he wanted a sky-blue version or crimson or ocher. By the mid-eighteenth century one proposal for a large garden in England had a drawing of a "chinees temple wing'd with umbrellas to shade the Auricula."

Logan also wants seeds of the "best" carnations and "Best double Holyhocks various colors, Several sorts of stocks, Hepatica, Dbl China Pinks, Snap Dragon, Catipellars & Snales."

Like John Bartram with Peter Collinson, William Logan exchanged plants with friends and merchants in England at the same time. He sent his friend the botanist John Blackburne cuttings, roots, seeds, and bulbs, as well as mockingbirds, flying squirrels, rabbits ("the rabbit all dead but one,") turtles, butterflies, beetles, and other American

"Exoticks." He offered to send larks after they were "settled in their cage."

Deborah Norris Logan's family had a city garden that was lush with fruits and herbs and flowers when she was a girl. Her house stood at the edge of the city, and when she looked westward out of the windows she could see pastures and the trees of Penn's woods. Her father, Charles Norris, had grown up at Fairhill; his brother Isaac Jr. lived there after his father's death. Isaac grew fig trees and vines in the garden and farmed the land like his father. He grafted cherries, and James Alexander at Springettsbury grafted orange stocks for him.

"I have," he wrote to Norris, "drawn myself entirely out of all trades and now live downright in the country way. My great business in the summer is my meadows and fences, opening my woods into groves, enlarging my fish ponds and beautifying my springs."

His brother had chosen to live on the edge of Philadelphia next to the statehouse.

Deborah Logan writes:

> Let me here just commemorate the pleasant view from the back parlour, its western window looking on a beautiful enclosure, separated from the pavement and gravelled lane, by a palisade adorned with scarlet honey-suckles, sweet briars, and roses, and shaded by fine spreading Catalpa's. The large willows which flourished at the bottom of the garden were the first of the species here, having been taken in a state that gave marks of vegetation, out of a hamper on a wharf at Boston, by Dr. Franklin, who brought them to Philadelphia and presented them to my Aunt Debby Norris, as one of the most successful cultivators that he knew.

There were large trees and white garden seats and a small apiary: "But the garden yet remains to be described—a spot of elegance and floral beauty. It was laid out in square Parterres and beds, regularly intersected by graveled and grass walks and alleys, yet some of the latter were so completely hid by the trees by which they were bordered as to be secluded and rural." The garden must have been mysterious and cool in the heat of midsummer. The weeping willows, the bright flowers bordered with paths of gravel, the shiny white benches. Deborah doesn't mention walking in the garden or sitting under the cool shade of one of the trees. She continues,

> A green bank with flights of stone steps, led the way into the garden, and a profusion of beautiful flowers and shrubs first met the view. The western part was more irregular, and contained on a high dry spot facing the south, and defended from the north by a high board fence, the hot-beds and seed-house, and led to a very shaded walk reaching to the extremity of the grounds, with vines, covering the fence, of the finest sort of grapes, and hid the other side from the rest of the garden by a continuation of espaliers in the most flourishing condition.

The greenhouse faced south and contained "the best collection of exotics in the Province at that period. It was well contrived, for the entrance into its stove was in a corner of the kitchen chimney, and a few chunks of hickory wood put into it at bed-time prevented any danger from the frost. The hot-house, for the mansion had a pretty little one, was the first of its kind in our city, where excellent Pineapples used to be raised."

Her family cultivated and dried "ample quantities of herbs" and gave them away to the sick in winter.

When she was twenty she married George Logan and moved to Stenton, where she had her own greenhouse and a farm of about five hundred acres. Like her grandfather Isaac, she was delighted with "nature in its rough dress."

# 34. Violets

JUST DOWN THE STREET from us on the way to the river is an optimistic field. Someone has planted slips of forsythia in a row along two edges and four or five tiny white pine trees in a grid in the center of the rectangular lot.

I've watched this patch of land since we moved here, vowing that I'd find out who the owner was and ask if I could plant a garden there. I want an orchard and a walk of pleached hornbeam and a square of tulips bordered by boxwood trees. But someone has beaten me to it. The wildflowers are mown now but a few days ago violets and the new slim leaves of chives poked up in a bed of heal-all.

Once I gathered buckets of violets so a friend could make them into jam. When I got married she sent a jar of the violet jelly as a wedding present. The jar sat in my refrigerator for years, a distilled memory of tromping around on the banks above the Mississippi one spring many years ago.

Violets and chives were cultivated in medieval gardens. My long garden on the side of the house reminds me of what those gardens must have been like. I don't have much room in the raised bed. It's about two feet wide and the length of the house. Most of my flowers and herbs were grown in the herbers of stately homes and castles and the yards of cottages from 1000 to 1500: a pink rose with five simple petals, tall flag iris, red and white columbines, red lilies, feverfew, mint, ivy, pinks, narcissus, pansies, honeysuckle, white Canterbury bells, and daylilies. The gardens were small enclosed plots with raised turf benches, or a fountain of shimmering water, or a curved arbor covered with grape leaves. Graveled paths led between green turf dotted with violets or daisies. There was usually an orchard. Fruit trees were planted for both their blossoms and their fruit. Lists include cherry, pear, apple, peach, medlar, quince, and plum. Ornamental trees were planted on hills or in rows across fields because they were beautiful and their shade was therapeutic. The elms or oaks or rows of ash were admired for their leaf and color. John Harvey in his book *Mediaeval Gardens* writes of "a mediaeval determination to find both beauty and utility in all the works of the creator."

In England kings had market gardens, and sometimes their gardeners sold the excess fruit and vegetables under the windows of the castle's chapel. Harvey mentions that account rolls for the royal residencies record that in 1264 the king ordered one hundred pear saplings for one of his gardens from a nursery in Oxford. The following year he could enjoy the white flowers of all those trees in the warm spring after a dark winter.

In the spring of 1275, William le Gardener bought quarts of lily bulbs, peony roots, white roses, and sage plants for a garden at the Tower of London.

I have a print of a painting that hangs in the Philadelphia Museum of Art. It's a painting of Saint Catherine of Alexandria from the late 1400s. She's standing on the Emperor Maxentius's back. His red booted feet stick out under her ermine-bordered dress; his head is at the corner of the painting just above the turf. Around her bends a garden. Beyond the edge of the garden is a moat and a castle with blue turrets and a clock tower, and beyond that are the hills planted with perfectly shaped trees in full leaf. Two swans float motionless in the moat. It's early summer. The red roses along the wall behind her spread their petals to the sun that paints the new leaves of a tree near the moat. Saint Catherine stands in front of a brick turf bench where a dandelion is blooming. At her feet near the emperor's arm are daisies. He strokes a plantain with his fingers.

The painter has transported her from the fourth century, when she lived and died, to his present, the late fifteenth century. Her golden hair ripples across her spare shoulders; she's reading a book. A noble girl who wouldn't marry the emperor because she was a bride of Christ, she disputed with fifty philosophers about Christianity against Maxentius, who was persecuting Christians. They tried to break her on a wheel, and when that didn't work, they beheaded her. Milk flowed from her severed head.

In the painting she holds a section of the wheel like a staff, resting her long fingers lightly on the wood.


The lilies of the gardens of the Middle Ages were white, the velvet trumpets of Madonna lilies. They bloomed in summer with red and white roses, the long spikes of lavender, the open mouths of the foxgloves.

My small backyard is like a tiny medieval courtyard. The spires of foxgloves display their little bells of mauve and cream. Periwinkle grows here like it grew in those gardens long ago, blooming now and again. My holly trees grew there, too, food for those birds who flew into those magical gardens that no longer exist.

# 35. *Catkins*

I'M READING DEBORAH LOGAN'S DIARIES. She was about twenty years younger than William Bartram and lived on the farm at Stenton, James Logan's place, from the time of her marriage in 1781 to her death in 1839.

Thomas Jefferson called James Logan's grandson George, Deborah's husband, the best farmer in Pennsylvania, both in theory and practice. I went into his stone barn a while ago. It was very large and cool on a hot day. It looked like a fortress with narrow slits in the sides. The farm, once five hundred acres, is now a park of about three.

For most of the time Deborah lived at Stenton, she was surrounded by large estates like Fairhill or smaller farms where farmers cultivated crops like potatoes, tobacco, and turnips in the fertile soil. After 1835, a railroad line ran through the property. The landscape of cultivated fields and the remnants of Penn's woods disappeared.

Like Bartram's Garden, Stenton is a green refuge in an area of crumbling warehouses and rows of two-story brick houses missing windows or doors built at the turn of the twentieth century. The day I was there, black plastic bags were piled along a rusty fence that bordered the property. Volunteers had cleaned up some of the trash along the sidewalks surrounding the house. I didn't notice the smokestacks or the roar of cars beyond the grassy few acres. I walked through the colonial revival garden with its old boxwood border and admired the tall magnolia tree, thick with shiny leaves by the edge of the greenhouse. Pink windflowers bloomed in the ordered squares of the garden.

Unlike Ann Bartram, Deborah Logan wrote for almost forty years about her life on the farm on the hill north of Philadelphia. I know quite a bit about her as I walk through her kitchen and into the greenhouse where, one night, the rats toppled over her plants. The long room faces southeast and has a wall of windows filled with geraniums. William Logan nursed his lemon and orange trees here through the winters.

In the main house sun streams through large windows. At night the shutters are closed tight with one round hole for light. Her bedroom has brown checked fabric and an upholstered commode. In one of the large rooms on the first floor a small yellow chair that was Deborah's sits near James Logan's crutches, propped against a tea table.

Her three sons were born one after the other in the first three years of her marriage. Her only surviving son, Albanus, inherited Stenton at her death, and his wife, Maria, gave the seventeen volumes of Deborah's journal to the Historical Society. I sit in the cool, dark reading room, not far from where she grew up, and listen to her voice on the page. Her diary is full of introspection and curiosity about the natural world.

I carefully turn page after page of the thick paper in her leather bound books: "Four years beyond half a century & good for so little," she writes in 1815.

After reading a description of the abyss seen from the top of Table Mountain in South Carolina, she imagines her death. "It suggested," she notes, "a most awful and sublime idea to my mind of the state of the human soul at the moment it is disengaged from the body, standing alone on the confines of a boundless eternity, where the scene opening on the astonished faculties . . . is no longer graduated by a reference to distances with which it has been familiar but immensity is at once spread before her."

She looked carefully at the wild woods around her. In late August one year she traveled with her husband to New Brunswick, New Jersey, the time "best for Botanical researches." She described a patch of orchids with orange flowers. And another flower that grew "from a small fibrous root three stalks—about 6 or 8 inches in length of a pale green, with small leaves on the stalks, to which eleven flowers were suspended, the size of a globe amaranthus and exactly the shape & appearance of it, only of a very deep gold colour."

Her husband, a doctor, takes her to the ocean and she drinks sea water for her stomach to make him happy. She rereads her diaries and writes a note at the bottom of a page after her husband's death: the "dearest, best beloved, of men, kindest, and most affectionate of Husbands."

One day she "clear-starched" and ironed, another she struggled with writing sonnets. She whitewashes the house and records the anniversary of her dear son Gustavas's death. She reassures her other two sons that their "welfare is one of the first desires of her heart."

She teaches domestic skills to a succession of girls and is "busy in the cellar getting the pork put away."

"I got very much out of humour with Anne," she notes, "for her neglect of her dairy utensils. I had them however, all thoroughly scoured and cleansed, and was reconciled upon her promise to do better."

She is precise and generous and proud. She copies letters from Jefferson to her husband in the pages of her journal and notes the arrival of "Buonaparte" in Philadelphia, a man of great wealth who was once favored by his famous brother.

I'm charmed by Deborah's attention to the small details of her life, and it's this skill that gets her through several difficult years. She loses her father, mother, brother, son, husband.

Delighted by the violent changes in the weather, the small movements of the animals on her farm, she continues to write. In March one year there were rats in the greenhouse and partridges in "coops just inside the door. One was still flying about and running up the trees from which he has thrown an abundance of leaves and lemons."

A squirrel moves her "young family" as she watches, "from a tree by the Spring House, to a Hollow Buttonwood, having previously carried leaves to line her apartment and make them a Bed."

One year, she is busy writing a paper on raising silkworms.

Like William Bartram she records the seasons on the farm, "the primary planets in direct line from each other—Venus, Jupiter, & Mars."

She notices the details of clouds and the cerulean color of the sky. "We have become very fond of Astronomy lately, but without the means of improving ourselves, or any Philosophical apparatus," she writes.

Sometimes May has an abundance of cherries, but her mind is uneasy: "If I were to keep a diary of my mind how often should I have to notice such a dry arid state."

Deborah notes with surprise the variations in the weather. October 1815 has "some Hoar frosts and the nights cold, but at this time warm and Hazy like what we call Indian summer. Prodigious flocks of Robins are about eating the Cedar berries & chirping like the spring."

Her greenhouse is warmed by wood but the calla is destroyed by cold on the twenty-seventh of December. She writes that she preserves her greenhouse plants only with difficulty. The sun is clear and splendid but the air very cold.

Dry, cold weather lasts all one spring: "We have now got beyond the middle of 5th m with a succession of weather very little like what we expect in the Spring. So dry it has been during the present and most of the last month, that vegetation suffers exceedingly, the grass is scanty beyond any thing usual at this season, and the seeds committed to the ground want moisture to vegetate. Last week we had some frosty nights, some of them black."

By late July, though, the early potatoes are uncommonly good, large and mealy, and they have the finest crop of large onions she can remember. Their wheat is also good.

George Logan died in early spring in 1821, and Deborah lived for almost twenty years after his death. She called the place where he was buried her "Inclosure" and designed a garden around the grave. Her journal for the year of his death is relentless and specific. She watches him die at the same time her dear niece Debby is near death. Doctors come and go, Debby is bled. Her husband is lightheaded and delirious. She writes in the spring of 1821, "My beloved husband will die. I feel his failure step by step."

Paragraphs are crossed out on almost every page of this volume of her journal. What's hidden under the careful circular erasures? Did someone else cross out line after line after her death?

"Oh my best loved and dearest earthly treasure, in thy loss, and in the severing of a union of nearly forty years, I feel that the world has nothing more to offer me, since I have lost thee! I never found my pen so inadequate to express what I have felt."

That spring followed a fall that was one of the most plentiful she ever saw—"everything that could bear fruit has been laden with it, even the cedar trees and bushes are fuller of berries than usual."

The cold came early and the turnip crop was still in the field on the frozen ground, the apples still ungathered.

She had, she writes, "a sense of loneliness in my heart that nothing in the world will ever eradicate."

In August, it is twenty-one years since her son Gustavus's death. The pain, she writes, has dimmed with time.

On the last page of this diary she pins a small piece of paper to the page:

> a memoranda of the desolate state of my mind, and present situation, but too faithfully represented by the closing season, the spring and summer of life, with their beauteous decorations, and agreeable fruits, are past—and what can I now look forward to with any anticipation of enjoyment?
>
> ... There seems to be nothing in store for me in this world, but what will lose by comparison with the Past ... I am now seated sorrowfully by myself in the Parlour which was wont to be called his. The vacant chair opposite to me where he used to sit.

A practicing Quaker, she consoles herself with the thought that her husband proclaimed himself a Christian at his death and that they will meet again in eternal life.

One January a few years later, she sits by the fire in the library with her pets, a parrot and a mockingbird, her sons away. She's in debt and melancholy.

But by spring she is comforted by the miraculous details of the earth. She writes: "The first indications of spring: the willow has put out wonderfully since the day before yesterday, and this morning my son brought me boughs from the hazel bushes full of long blossoms (Catkins). It is odd that this little nut takes so long a time to perfect its fruit when the Walnuts and the Chestnut do not blossom 'till it is late in the season. But divine wisdom orders all aright."

# 36. Honeysuckle

IN JULY, MY GARDEN IN THE CITY is a modest collection of pleasant, common flowers, their petals open to the thick humid air that hangs like cotton above their heads. All the petals and tendrils, the curling tips of vines, unfurl in a delicate gesture all over the garden.

I like the mysterious way leaves sometimes turn into twining arms and the way the passion flower moves in a dance on the wall toward the invisible fishing line suspended from the lattice.

"Plants," Peter Bernhardt writes in *The Rose's Kiss*, "tend to require a rhythmic, repetitive cycle over a period of weeks or months before they make buds or become ready to open them. This period, in which the plant's physiology must follow the rhythm of the cue, is known as entrainment. Eventually, flower development becomes synchronized with one or more cues that are repeated every twenty-four hours."

Daylilies, large bright orange flowers with red throats and flaring orange and yellow pistils, and a smaller version with pointed petals, open one by one, their bloom the end of their long dance of cues. What I think of as wild daylilies are blooming now, too, their interior ragged and furled. They were some of the first plants the settlers cultivated, familiar and beautiful, reminding them of home. In China they were cultivated for food, and the buds were ground into a powder that could banish grief.

My small gardens are not quite like the gardens that grew in the ancient cities of Greece and in Rome and Alexandria, though I like to think my potted orange tree and little boxwood were cultivated there. Excavations of cities buried by the eruption of Vesuvius in 79 AD have shown that most private houses had at least one garden, a corner of the courtyard set aside for planting. Even blocks of flats had window boxes so small, Maureen Carroll writes in *Earthly Paradises*, that one writer of the period said a cucumber could not lie straight.

The gardens in Roman cities were irrigated by a system of aqueducts. In Pompeii gardens lay at the back of the house, an enclosed yard for growing vegetables, fruits, and herbs. The larger houses had an inner courtyard that was sometimes bigger than the area of the house, a peristyle garden. This was a pleasure garden for walking in the shade. Most of these courtyards had a central garden for flowers, a fountain, and a pool. The garden in the House of the Vettii in Pompeii has a covered walkway surrounding a garden open to the sun and rain. There are white stone benches and round pools with tall grass growing on the edge. Flowers and herbs and vegetables are planted in curving rows around the perimeter of the courtyard. It is useful and serene.

The long narrow garden bed along my house is cool and dappled under the light of the two elms even in the heat of July. I like to think it's like walking past a woodland garden, the hot breeze pushing the striped lilies this way and that. The garden is all greens and pinks, the pointed red-veined leaves of cannas poking up near lavender and a chartreuse and yellow grass. Unlike the gardens of Pompeii, my garden adorns the outside of my house. I don't plant anything too expensive or tricky there. Sometimes someone will snip a lily or sit on a patch of impatiens to eat lunch. A long time ago, before we lived here, neighbors say that someone hid a gun in the ivy.

Honeysuckle crawls up the stucco wall on invisible threads tied to the deck. A clematis, deep purple, blooms at the very top of the long window for a second time this summer. There's a wild pink rose and zinnias about to bloom, red salvia, chocolate mint, and green mint. The sunflowers bend over the sidewalk. I water the garden with a long green hose and a plastic watering can.

Greek cities relied on rivers for water and were intensively built, with no space for gardens. A green belt of groves of trees and garden plots followed the river outside of town. In the fourth century BC, gardens in Athens were a luxury. Carroll notes that Plato bought a garden in the suburbs in 388 BC for two thousand drachmas. The average daily wage was one drachma. Plato had to be very rich to buy his garden. Epicurus paid eight thousand drachmas for his garden in the suburbs.

Gardeners were careful about what kind of water they used on their plants. Each source—springs, rivers, and canals—was different. Onions needed clean, cold water. Most herbs were watered twice a day, but basil was watered three times.

The tasks of the gardener in the ancient world were like my tasks as the gardener of my small gardens, but a bit more complicated. I have no employer. The job description of one gardener called Peftumont written by the owner of the garden, Talames, in the late part of the third century AD is recorded on a jar in Egypt: "Peftumont is required to water the garden and maintain its irrigation channels; to make four baskets of palm fibre for earth; to protect the garden against sparrows and crows and to complete his work at the end of each day." He was also required to show his excrement to Talames at the end of each day to prove he had not eaten the produce.

A flourishing garden in antiquity was a holy place. Graves were erected in enclosed gardens. Both the living and the dead enjoyed the beauty of the cool green enclosure. In the fifth century BC tomb gardens in Alexandria were planted with cabbage, asparagus, leeks, grapes, and date palms.

Gardens and groves were often destroyed by attacking armies in part because they were a mysterious symbol of power.

One single large white lily, a deeply perfumed Casa Blanca, has just opened in my garden. It's secret and powerful. As big as a small melon and just as sweet smelling with large curved waxy petals. Huge rust-colored anthers balance on delicate green filaments, and the interior is spotted with raised greenish nubs and hairs of white flesh.

A garden painting from a house in Pompeii shows laurels and viburnum, roses, strawberry trees, oleanders, date palms, ivy, poppies, chamomile, violets, morning glories, and Madonna lilies. Even if your garden was too small to grow trees and lush vines you could commission an artist to paint your walls with lush plants and startling birds.

In my small courtyard, the pots of bamboo are still leafing out after the hard cold winter. Their light green stalks bend and the leaves wiggle in the hot air. We have just enough room for a small table and three chairs. Sometimes I stand in the center of my courtyard and drink my tea, watching the early light on the ferns and petals of the flowers.

On the deck a bee with black fur and gold legs harvests pollen from the cascading thyme in three big pots. Peter Bernhardt tells me that "some flowers with radial symmetry limit both the movement and the diversity of their pollinators by narrowing and lengthening the point of access. The bee that tramps all over the rose has only limited entry to morning glories (*Ipomoea*). She reaches the nectar at the base of the narrowing funnel of petals by pushing her head down the floral tube and lapping nectar with the 'spoon' that tips her elongated tongue."

This bee has bright yellow pollen on her legs, but other shades are common: mignonettes have blue pollen, lesser bindweed, black, tobacco flowers, tan. This bee is part of the richness of my small garden, harvesting pollen she then feeds to the brood.

I've been trying to nestle my plants in the kind of soil they like. I've added compost and humus, topsoil and potting soil. I prune their roots. Sometimes I coddle them with liquid fertilizer. I try to give the woodland plants a mulch of leaves I gather from our trees in the fall and spring, crumbling the leaves around their unfurling leaves or fronds.

In the community garden a few blocks away, a path of wood chips cuts the garden in half. At the end of the path is a little boxwood tree, vigorously sprouting. I'm letting it grow into a wild shape.

By 54 BC gardeners had attained professional status. If you wanted to you could become a topiary specialist, designing gardens with trees and bushes in geometrical patterns. Maureen Carroll writes that the *topiarius* evolved into an artist who clipped boxwood, ivy, laurel, cypress, myrtle, acanthus, dwarf plane trees, and rosemary into shapes: the gardener's name, fleets of ships, formal hedges.

Seedling tiger lilies line the front of the patch too young to bloom. Scott gathered the shiny brown seeds last summer in Vermont. Iris leaves bend this way and that under the tall stems of the sunflowers.

The garden looks cool even in the heat of midmorning, shaded by the tall arching branches of the sunflowers.

# 37. Franklinia

IN 1870 WILLIAM ROBINSON published a book called *The Wild Garden*. His idea of wild was not wilderness but a kind of ordered use of wild edges. He liked to fill meadows with spring flowers and harvest the useful hay later. He planted the edges of woods with drifts of lupines and lilies, the margins of roads with ferns. On old stumps and large trees he coaxed clematis and honeysuckle. I like one wild garden in particular where lilies bloom on the wet margins of a stream and huge magnolia blossoms fall on a winding grassy path, up the river from Bartram's Garden around the bend just outside of Philadelphia.

Mary Gibson Henry gardened here in the soil of an old Quaker farm for a good part of the twentieth century. She collected native plants. Inspired by William Bartram's book, she said she wanted one of the plants he described in his *Travels* that was no longer available to American collectors: *Rhododendron speciosum*, Oconee azalea. Bartram seemed to define her impulse when he wrote, "Whilst I, continually impelled by a restless spirit of curiosity, in pursuit of new productions of nature, my chief happiness consisted in tracing and admiring the infinite power, majesty, and perfection of the Great Almighty Creator, and in the contemplation, that through divine aid and permission, I might be instrumental in discovery, and introducing into my native country, some original productions of nature, which might become useful to society."

Mary Gibson Henry's husband was a doctor. She was a descendent of one of the first Quaker families to settle near Philadelphia. I've seen a photograph of her in a gown at the top of a staircase in the cool stone ballroom in her grandmother's house outside Philadelphia. She's dressed in a long black silk dress, daughters to her left and right in shimmering slips of gowns. On the floor is a lion's skin, the head facing the women on the marble steps.

For many years Mary Henry lived in Philadelphia. She had a small yard like ours and grew lilacs and bearded iris and narcissus. Her yard was big enough for a greenhouse, and she grew orchids there. She had five children. Her first day off, she wrote in her autobiography, was after nineteen years of marriage.

In 1926 the Henrys bought land just outside Philadelphia on a hill above the river in Gladwyne, where they built a house and a large greenhouse. And then her youngest son died. Many years later she wrote, "Great grief came to us in 1927, when we lost our youngest son, aged six. I craved solitude and working with my plants was all I cared to do."

It's fall and we're taking a guided walk in Mary Gibson Henry's garden. Her granddaughters are leading us up to the rock garden and down through the thick woods to the sparkling streams that Mrs. Henry describes in her autobiography. Perhaps all gardens are built on grief. That impulse to make something beautiful out of the slippery stuff that crumbles away as you pat and water each plant. Graham runs up the grassy slope looking for jungle plants, all the way to the outcrop Mary Henry exposed on the crest of her hill above her house.

"Excuse me," he says to Betsey, one of Mary Henry's granddaughters. "Do you have any carnivorous plants here?"

"No," she says. "But a botanist who was here a few days ago told us about some plants in the Amazon that eat small children, or at least small animals."

Mary Gibson Henry writes in her autobiography that she "fell in love" at seven with the tiny *Linnaea borealis* ssp. *americana*, the twinflower, delicate and pink nodding above shiny evergreen leaves.

Even though she was a "city girl" she "loved the outdoors." In 1908 she climbed Mont Blanc with her brother and three guides. After her children were old enough she started collecting native plants and spent the rest of her life consumed by her garden. She traveled in a specially outfitted car—with an "attic," an electrically lit desk, and a bookcase. The rear compartment was "insulated and ventilated so that newly collected plants travel comfortably. Three plant presses, numerous buckets, spades, etc.," were part of the equipment. Her chauffeur was also her gardener.

She traveled twenty-five hundred miles in her car and on foot to find a *Rhododendron speciosum*, a native azalea with deep orange blossoms. She scoured first the coastal plain, retracing the Bartrams' steps and then up into the Piedmont. In the swamps of the southeast coast she found red lilies and *Hymenocallis*, spiderlilies, "like great exotic butterflies, snow-white and marvelously fragrant." She was horrified when she saw the delicate wetlands trampled by cattle, or places where ranchers had dug water holes or filled the watery ground and used it as a dump.

On one of her journeys to the eastern slopes of the Appalachian Mountains, "so beautiful and so enormously interesting," she and her daughter Josephine were "held up by three men with rifles, who threatened us roughly."

In 1931 she made the first of several trips to British Columbia with her husband and four children, looking for a tropical valley that was a blank on every map.

In the wild north "Polemoniums, Delphiniums, Mertensias and Penstemons grew in undreamed of profusion." They rode "for miles and miles through meadows so blue they looked like bits of fallen sky."

She made three more trips with Josephine. They shot bears and camped out in a large canvas tent. Once they lost most of their food in a flooded river while fording the water on logs lashed together with ropes. They gathered *Allium schoenoprasum* ssp. *sibiricum* and flavored their meals with the slim green chives. On one of their trips they sent twelve carrier pigeons back home to Dr. Henry to let him know how they were doing. She had a mountain named after her in northern British Columbia and mapped parts of northwest Canada when the topographer accompanying them got sick. She loved being in the far north. She was small and slim and traveled on a horse that sometimes slipped on the shifting talus of the mountains. Her horse carried "plant press, rifle, camera, fishing equipment, my precious spade, cans of living plants, etc."

Mary and her daughter rode their horses 460 miles along game trails above the timberline or through the thick forests. "Often at night the wolves howled about our tents," she writes in her autobiography, "and I loved these eerie sounds."

She collected over 350 flowering plants and ferns on her expeditions to the north. In her travels she found *Rhododendron lapponicum*, Lapland rosebay, near St Paul's lake in British Columbia, a surprising discovery in the West.

She planted a large collection of native plants in the "Wild Garden" at Gladwyne.

"Wading," she wrote, "usually barelegged, through countless rattlesnake-infested swamps add[s] immensely to the interest of the day's work. On several occasions I have been so deeply mired I had to be pulled out."

In a cow pasture in Alabama near the Gulf of Mexico she found a sweet yellow lily and collected seeds from the blossom. The plant turned out to be a new discovery, and in five years the seeds bloomed. She named the lily *Lilium iridollae*, "the pot of gold at the foot of her rainbow."

I walk behind Fielding Howe. His name is stitched into his pants at the belt and a little scarf is tied in a bow at his neck.

"Great day," he yelled as he drove up in his car, his gray head craning out the window. He's the official ornithologist for the Henry Foundation but today he can't seem to see his birds. In 1999 he counted 96 robins here, 48 barn swallows, 29 Carolina chickadees, 30 dark-eyed juncos, 11 eastern bluebirds, 2 field sparrows, 2 red-bellied woodpeckers, 3 red-tailed hawks, 2 ruby-crowned kinglets, and many other species for a total of 510 birds. The deer are fenced out, as they nibble the sweet shoots.

We've circled past a huge bronze hickory.

"We had one you could see from the highway," Scott says.

"My grandmother when she was eighty could do more pushups than my younger brother, and he was very athletic," Betsey says as we wind our way through the garden. "She hired Susan and me to weed and paid us minimum wage. My aunt weeded fourteen hours a day here. I looked up an old woman who had known my grandmother and showed her a picture of the hickory—'Oh that's the sapling from Uncle Henry's hunting lodge, under water now in Virginia,' she told me."

Graham picks up a huge magnolia leaf and a shiny seed, "like wood," he says. "And look, someone tried to nibble it and then dropped it."

I've seen trees like these in the woods in the Carolinas and Georgia, large magnolias with shiny green leaves in January. We drove there on our way to Florida not long ago, and I imagined William Bartram, ecstatic, traveling under so much sky through deep shiny woods skirting marshes where, once he got to Florida, alligators lived. We went south, as he did, from Philadelphia and all its commerce to the wild edge of the coastal plain. We had driven there to spend Christmas with my mother, who lives a bit south of where Bartram spent his time on the St. Johns River.

The last time I went to Florida in a car, I was a few years older than when I made my first garden. The highways were not finished then and the roads ran over old bridges in cypress swamps, the limbs bristly with Spanish moss. We watched children our age in the dusty red fields standing near the small wooden houses without windows where they lived. We were on our way south in the spring to spend a week by the ocean. When we drove north from there this winter, I noticed the change in the air from Florida to South Carolina, the sweet fragrant breeze of Florida dissipated in the air of the Carolinas, and then the marshes, great advances of gray-green marsh grass along the edges of the sea, the pines, sharp and pungent, and the long beaches where Bartram road his horse home that last time. How beautiful it must have been, I thought, as we made our way north in a line of cars through the cities one by one to Philadelphia.

When I was nine and made my first garden in my Aunt Eva's backyard I had no idea I would live anywhere else. I was on my first big voyage by myself. A little girl with dark hair crouched under the cool shade of shiny trees, the sweet sharp smell of lemon surrounding me as I worked. I was mostly playing. But I had never been anywhere so fruitful and fragrant. The wide brown leaves that made boats for my dolls were perhaps the fallen leaves of magnolias. There may have been bougainvillea and bottle brush trees and banana trees near my garden. What was most exotic, though, was the light, hot and broken by leaves and limbs in the backyard and sweet and yellow like the lemons, tasty like the oranges.

Here some magnolias lose their leaves and grow furry pointed buds that I feel I could suck like the tips of some kind of fruit. We examine sassafras, sarsaparilla, holly, magnolia, yucca, Franklinia. "The flowers must be seen from above," Susan, Mary Henry's other granddaughter, says.

The Franklinia is a direct descendent of a tree that grew in the wild. William Bartram collected the seeds when he was traveling in the swampy lands of Georgia and Florida. He planted it in his father's greenhouse when he returned to Philadelphia in 1777. His father died before the shrub bloomed. Its flowers are "very large, expand themselves perfectly, are of a snow-white colour, and ornamented with a crowen or tassel of gold coloured refulgent stamina in their center" and smell like oranges. William and his father had first seen the "very curious tree" eight years before he collected the seeds. These seeds are the source of all the Franklinia trees growing in gardens today. No one has ever seen *Franklinia alatamaha* growing in the wild since then.

How beautiful, I think, it must have been here when there were woods like these with all their tall and curious trees growing along the river until you came to marshes spreading out in a vast delta at the mouth of the Delaware, salty and fertile.

"My grandmother dug some of the soil out after she went to Edinburgh and saw how they made their rock gardens there, and carted gravel in where she planted the plants she collected from all over North America, especially the Texas Panhandle," Susan tells us.

Mary Henry explains in *Herbertia*: "It has been a surprising but alloyed joy to see these plants from the wild making themselves at home. To be sure, I always try to give them a comfortable spot and a suitable soil mixture and spare no effort on their behalf ... Magnolias, Halesias, Rhododendrons, Liliums, Hymenocallis, Trilliums, Alliums, Phlox, Liatris, Penstemons and Yuccas are my special favorites."

She had a "tiny" greenhouse that kept her busy in the winter and six cold frames. She cultivated almost six hundred pots of amaryllids and was involved in a "serious breeding program" of her favorite genus, *Cyrtanthus*.

Now red-tailed hawks and turkey vultures fly so close we can see their naked heads. An animal Graham and I can't identify, something that looks like a cross between a mouse and chipmunk—at first I think it's a vole—hops under logs and the layered carcasses of leaves. The mockingbirds are singing their heads off.

I admire the purple berries, red berries, the burnished leaves of the bushes. Graham runs in the piles of the crispy large magnolia leaves, circles like a dog around and around. We wind through the woods on little trails, one Henry granddaughter behind us, one in front. The garden almost wasn't here at all. In 1949 the state wanted to dump "silt, sewage, and refuse" pumped from the Schuylkill on the site of the garden. Botanists lobbied the governor to save the garden, calling it "as important as the Royal Botanic Garden at Kew."

Betsey told me that the garden consumes her. She lives on the property in a cottage near the barn and hasn't had time to mow her lawn in four years. The plumbing in the house needs work. The deer fence has holes in it. When her Aunt Josephine was the director of the garden she let things go. There were beer parties in the rock garden.

I've seen Mary Henry's daughter Josephine driving a small dark car fast up the long drive to the house and garden at Gladwyne. Her hair was long and white, and she wore a bright red dress.

Mary Gibson Henry died when she was eighty-two. She had been told to live a less-strenuous life by her doctor. When she died she was collecting plants in North Carolina. Mary Harrison writes in an article in *Arnoldia* that in the last year of her life Mary Henry spent forty-two days in the field collecting seventy-five plants and filled orders for plants that she sent all over the world from her garden at Gladwyne. There were over a thousand different species of woody plants in her wild garden.

Even in the winter the witch-hazel in her garden has blossoms on bare branches—*Hamamelis virginiana* var. *henryae* and *Hamamelis vernalis* on sunny days. Sharp as lemon rind, they are the first plants collected by John Bartram near the source of the Schuylkill in the

Blue Mountains in 1736 and cultivated in English shrubbery and wilderness and along woods walks in the eighteenth century.

I often walk in the Azalea Garden near my house on the edge of the river. It's part of the original waterworks garden, the edge of Springettsbury below Fair Mount. Not wild like the Henry Foundation's garden, it's clipped and manicured. This garden has a Franklinia tree, too, another descendent of the original seeds gathered by William Bartram on his long journey over two hundred years ago.

I like this garden best in the very early spring when the buds of the rhododendrons and azaleas are demure and shut tight and the tiny fat blooms of the snowdrops open their small cups to the warming air.

# 38. Carnations

MY SON WAS CONFIRMED in the Catholic church yesterday. I arranged the flowers on the altar with Ronnie. It's a fiction, after all, that time is moving slowly here in Philadelphia. I've been through whole leaps of time since we crossed the threshold into this house built on the rocks that once were the foundation of another garden. Graham is taller than I am.

My tiny columbine is edged out by heuchera and mint. The bamboo died this winter, a harsh one for Philadelphia. I have a lush bed of daylilies and three new lilies: *Lilium henryi*, Asiatic citronella, and snow queen. I've planted *Galtonia candicans*, the summer hyacinth—a very tall plant with white bells suspended from a thick stem, the bells dipped in green like snowdrops, a gladiolus called wig's sensation, flame red, and three kinds of dahlias. A vine that's beautiful and poisonous, *Gloriosa superba*, refuses to poke up its head in the big pot on the deck.

In my small courtyard we've planted a delicately beautiful Japanese maple in a whiskey barrel and a tiny banana plant in a pot.

A passion vine with red flowers is shooting up the lattice on the back wall of the patio, and a wisteria climbs toward my neighbor's porch.

The honeysuckle is finally blooming, after several years, in long, twisted streamers on the side of the house, held up by invisible threads of fishing line. Earthworms have appeared mysteriously in the side bed. Dragonflies dip and hover over the blossoms. A praying mantis clings to the narrow leaves of striped daylilies on the deck.

One of my neighbors told me that Mary Robinson has sold her

house. She can't get up and down the stairs anymore. Father Alberto went back to Spain.

My flowers on the altar were beautiful carnations, blood red, and lacy white larkspur and tight red berries held above the tip of the bishop's miter as he anointed my child with the fire of the Holy Spirit. Go out and be brave like the saints, he told the children gathered in their red robes.

We were all at the edge of the coastal plain on the first step of the Piedmont as we watched the children ascend the white marble steps to the altar, and the Schuylkill made its way to the ocean in a curve just around the corner. A starling fed her baby in a nest tucked in the eaves of the church.

# 39. Strawberry

I CAN PUT MY FINGER ON THE PLACE where the Labyrinthine Garden stood on a copy of a map from 1833 that sits on my desk. The engraver has written "Pagoda" and circled the word. The pagoda sits in the middle of the outline of the labyrinth on the spot where I now live. Across the street from the garden to the north there are no cross streets, but south, a canal and the proposed route of a railroad line cut through the grid of streets. Pratt's garden is noted on the river and the Fair Mount Water Works is drawn with three pools at the top of the hill. A narrow stream flows to the river from the east and south of the pagoda. The Schuylkill is a dark curve on the top of the map. The penitentiary is drawn like a flower encased in a square, the petals the solitary wings of the building.

My shrub roses are starting to bloom in mid-May, and the green tips of the lilies I planted a week ago are already popping up in the dirt like the tips of asparagus. When it rains the silver drops roll off the fern fronds to the slate below. Sometimes I watch the small movement of leaf and stem in the slight breeze. The banana leafs out one blade at a time, unfolding a larger version of the shiny green flat leaf from the center. The Japanese maple bends, its leaves like delicate hands.

I like the idea that I'm cultivating a garden here in the middle of our lives, curled and wandering eventually to the heart of the labyrinth. All gardens lead here for me.

It's going to be hot today, near ninety. Perhaps on this kind of day, the heat would have been enough to lure lots of people out of the city and up to my hill where they would sip cool drinks and climb to the top of the pagoda with its painted bells and wind their way through the green labyrinth under tall trees, smelling the sweet roses and peonies that lined the edges of the garden. And then they'd have ice cream and strawberries, perhaps in fruit by now if the spring was very hot. They could see the curving river from the pagoda and the whole city fanning out below them.

The river would be cool still, like the water in our taps, and carp might be spawning. And just like my trees breathing their cool breath into my face, the trees that shimmered in the heat would be shedding mist and air into the faces of those men and women and children playing in the labyrinth on that hot spring day.

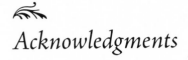

# Acknowledgments

THANKS TO Maddy Blais, Nicole Greaves-Dougherty, Karen Donovan, Ann de Forest, Chris Jerome, Sharon Kirsch, Carolyn Raskin, and Joanne Wyckoff for their comments on this book and for their support. Special thanks to Elaine Terranova for her encouragement and advice. Ted Kerasote helped with this project (including the title we didn't use) and gave me the generous gift of a place to write in the past. Thanks to my colleagues at Temple, Dennis Lebofsky (whose postcards became a chapter), Eli Goldblatt, and Keith Gumery, for conversations about writing. Jane Alling at the Pennsylvania Horticultural Society was my guide to vanished gardens. My gardens in Philadelphia would vanish, too, without George Pahler, our neighbor and friend. Grace and Dick Caldwell made us feel like Philadelphia was home. My thanks to the Association of Writers and Writing Programs for the award in creative nonfiction and to Michael Martone for choosing my book. Thanks also to Regan Huff, Jennifer Reichlin, and the wonderful people at the University of Georgia Press, especially Stephen Barnett for his careful editing. I'm grateful to the Leeway Foundation and the Pennsylvania Council on the Arts for grants while I was writing this book. And, finally, thanks to Graham for coming along on so many walks through woods and gardens.

Chapter II, "Bamboo," appeared in *Isotope*, and sections of the first three chapters of the book appeared in a different form in *Garden Solutions*.

# Sources

SPRINGETTSBURY

### 3. Daffodil

Michael A. Godfrey discusses the geography of the Mid-Atlantic in *Field Guide to the Piedmont: The Natural Habitats of America's Most Lived-in Region, from New York City to Montgomery, Alabama* (Chapel Hill: University of North Carolina Press, 1997). The quotation from Galen on page 8 is from Claire Shaver Haughton's *Green Immigrants: The Plants that Transformed America* (New York: Harcourt, Brace, Jovanovich, 1978). A description of the poisonous qualities of daffodils is found in Charles Kingsley Levy and Richard B. Primack, *A Field Guide to Poisonous Plants and Mushrooms of North America* (Brattleboro, Vt.: The Stephen Greene Press, 1984). Two sources for information on the Lenape in Philaldephia are Paul A. W. Wallace, *Indians in Pennsylvania*, 2d ed. (Harrisburg: Pennsylvania Historical and Museum Commission, 1999), and James Wilson, *The Earth Shall Weep: A History of Native America* (New York: Atlantic Monthly Press, 1998).

### 4. Hornbeam

Allan W. Armstrong describes Peter Collinson in his introduction to *"Forget not Mee & My garden . . ." Selected Letters, 1725–1768, of Peter Collinson, F.R.S.* (Philadelphia: Memoirs of the American Philosophical Society, vol. 241, 2002). James Alexander's letters to Thomas Penn are on file at The Historical Society of Pennsylvania, Philadelphia. Thomas Penn's letters are also at The Historical Society. All of the letters of John and William Bartram that I discuss are found in *The Correspondence of John Bartram, 1734-1777*, ed. Edmund Berkeley and Dorothy Smith Berkeley (Gainesville: University Press of Florida, 1992). A biography of James Alexander is included in Whitfield J. Bell Jr., *Patriot-Improvers: Biographical Sketches of Members of the American Philosophical Society*, vol. 1 (Philadelphia: American Philosophical Society, 1997). Peter Kalm's descriptions of deer are in *Peter Kalm's Travels in North America* (New York: Dover, 1966). The quote from William Penn on page 16 is from Ann Leighton, *American Gardens of the Eighteenth Century: "For Use or for Delight"* (Amherst: University of Massachusetts Press, 1986). Quotations from Deborah Logan are from her unpublished diaries, 1815-1839, in The Historical Society of Pennsylvania. Many of the details of Thomas Penn's house and garden are described in Elizabeth McLean and Mark Reinberger, "Springettsbury, A Lost Estate of the Penn Family," *Journal of the New England Garden History Society* vol. 7 (fall 1999). Virgil is noted in John F. Watson's *Annals of Philadelphia and Pennsylvania: A Collection of Memoirs, Anecdotes, and Incidents of the City and Its Inhabitants and of the Earliest Settlements of the Inland Part of Pennsylvania from the Days of the Founders* (1857; RootsWeb.com).

## 5. Lemons

*Catalogue of Splendid and Rare Green House and Hot House Plants: To Be Sold by Auction, at Lemon Hill, Formerly the Seat of the Late Henry Pratt, Deceased, on Tuesday, the 5th day of June, 1838, and to Be Continued Daily Till Completed* by D. & C. A. Hill, Auctioneers (Philadelphia, 1838) lists plants for sale at Lemon Hill. Andrew Jackson Downing describes Lemon Hill in *Landscape Gardening and Rural Architecture* (New York: Dover Publications, 1991 [a version of *Treatise on the Theory and Practice of Landscape Gardening*]). The quotations that describe the gardens and buildings at Lemon Hill are in *Lemon Hill: In Its Connection With the Efforts of Our Citizens and Councils to Obtain a Public Park, Philadelphia, June 1856* (Philadelphia: Crissy & Markley, 1856).

## 7. Tulip Tree

Edgar Allan Poe, "Morning on the Wissahiccon," in *The Unabridged Edgar Allan Poe* (Philadelphia: Running Press, 1983).

## 8. Catalpa

The quote from Frances Trollope is in Jane Mork Gibson, "The Fairmount Waterworks," *Bulletin* (Philadelphia Museum of Art) 84, no. 360–61, (summer 1988). Ann Leighton describes the gardens at the waterworks in *American Gardens of the Nineteenth Century: For Comfort and Affluence* (Amherst: University of Massachusetts Press, 1987).

## 9. Water Lilies

My information on shad comes from Rich Remer, "Fishtown and the Shad Fisheries," *Pennsylvania Legacies* 2, no. 2 (November 2002).

## 10. Peony

Matthew Eli Baigell gives the details of Haviland's career in "John Haviland," PhD dissertation (University of Pennsylvania, 1965). The Group for Environmental Education, *Philadelphia Architecture: A Guide to the City* (Cambridge, Mass.: MIT Press for the Foundation for Architecture, 1984) mentions the contest for designing the prison. Thomas P. Slaughter in *The Natures of John and William Bartram* (New York: Vintage Books, 1997) was a source for the information about John and William Bartram in this chapter and several others.

## 11. Bamboo

Information on bamboo is in Emmet J. Judziewicz et al., *American Bamboos* (Washington, D.C.: Smithsonian Institution Press, 1999). The quotations from Koetsu are from Hon'ami Koetsu, *The Arts of Hon'ami Koetsu*, ed. Felice Fischer (Philadelphia: Philadelphia Museum of Art, 2000). The Spirn quotation about the tea ceremony is from *The Language of Landscape* (New Haven, Conn.: Yale University Press, 1998).

## 12. Thistle

Ann Leighton in *American Gardens of the Eighteenth Century* (1986) describes William Penn's plan for Philadelphia and his gardening methods. John R. Stilgoe discusses clearing land along the Delaware in *The Common Landscape of America, 1580 to 1845* (New Haven, Conn.: Yale University Press, 1982).

## 13. Snapdragon

Peter Kalm's observations of Bartram are from *Travels in North America*. Details of the history of flower arranging are from Mary Rose Blacker,

*Flora Domestica: A History of British Flower Arranging 1500-1930* (London: National Trust, 2000). Collinson's letters to Bartram are from *The Correspondence of John Bartram*. Ann Leighton discusses Bartram's flower experiments in *American Gardens of the Eighteenth Century* (1986).

## 14. Holly Tree

Information on Galileo is from Timothy Ferris, *Coming of Age in the Milky Way* (New York: Anchor Books, 1989), and Dava Sobel, *Galileo's Daughter: A Historical Memoir of Science, Faith, and Love* (New York: Penguin Books, 2000). The quote about quasars on page 70 is from Ferris, *Coming of Age*. Anne Whiston Spirn gives the history of Mill Creek in *The Granite Garden: Urban Nature and Human Design* (New York: Basic Books, 1984).

## 15. Elm

James H. Merrell describes Penn's woods in *Into the American Woods: Negotiators on the Pennsylvania Frontier* (New York: Norton, 1999). The letters of William Penn and his agent in Pennsylvania are in *The Papers of William Penn*, vol. 2, ed. Mary Maples Dunn and Richard S. Dunn (Philadelphia: University of Pennsylvania Press, 1982).

## 16. Skunk Cabbage

Kalm's description of the wildlife in Philadelphia can be found in his *Travels in North America*. "Fairmount Park Natural Lands Restoration Master Plan," Fairmount Park System, includes a discussion of the plants and animals in Fairmount Park.

### KINGSESSING

## 17. Pennyroyal

All letters to John Bartram in this chapter are in *The Correspondence of John Bartram*. Joel T. Fry lists the plants in Bartram's greenhouse and gives descriptions of medicinal plants in "John Bartram and His Garden: Would

John Bartram Recognize His Garden Today?" in *America's Curious Botanist: A Tercentennial Reappraisal of John Bartram 1699–1777*, ed. Nancy E. Hoffmann and John C. Van Horne (Philadelphia: American Philosophical Society, 2004). Details about the lives of women in this time period are in Joan M. Jenson, *Loosening the Bonds: Mid-Atlantic Farm Women, 1750–1850* (New Haven, Conn.: Yale University Press, 1980), and Laurel Thatcher Ulrich, *A Midwife's Tale: The Life of Martha Ballard, Based on Her Diary, 1785–1812* (New York: Knopf, 1990). Ann Leighton describes gardens during this time in *Early American Gardens: For Meate or Medicine* (1986). Martha Logan's letter to Ann Bartram is in the collection of The Historical Society of Pennsylvania. The letter from John to William is in the collection of the New York Historical Society, Bartram Folder. Frances Phipps gives a wealth of detail about the foods of the era in *Colonial Kitchens, Their Furnishings and Their Gardens* (New York: Hawthorn Books, 1972). Ann Bartram is discussed in Thomas P. Slaughter, *The Natures of John and William Bartram*, and Merril D. Smith, "The Bartram Women: Farm Wives, Artists, Botanists, and Entrepreneurs," *Bartram Broadside* (winter 2001).

## 18. Marsh Grass

Urban gardens are described in H. Patricia Hynes, *A Patch of Eden: America's Inner-City Gardeners* (White River Junction, Vt.: Chelsea Green, 1996). Information about pigeons is from Tina Kelley, "From Lowly Pigeon; In Study of Mating Habits, Third Graders Seek Key to the Diversity of a Species," *New York Times* (January 10, 2000). Susan Strasser gives details of nineteenth-century trash in *Waste and Want: A Social History of Trash* (New York: Holt, 2000).

## 19. Oranges

All the passages quoted are in William Bartram, *Travels of William Bartram*, ed. Mark Van Doran (New York: Dover, 1955). A description of William Bartram's travels is in Edmund Berkeley and Dorothy Smith Berkeley, *The Life and Travels of John Bartram from Lake Ontario to the River St. John* (Tallahassee: University Presses of Florida, 1982), and Thomas P. Slaughter, *The Natures of John and William Bartram*. Edward J. Cashin discusses Bartram's adventures in *William Bartram and the American Revolution on the Southern Frontier* (Columbia: University of South Carolina Press, 2000).

## 20. Wild Rice

Information about muskrats is from Charles Fergus, Wildlife of Pennsylvania and the Northeast (Mechanicsburg, Pa.: Stackpole Books, 2000), and Bruce Stutz, *Natural Lives, Modern Times: People and Places of the Delaware River* (New York: Crown, 1992). The details of bird migration are in Scott Weidensaul, *Living on the Wind: Across the Hemisphere with Migratory Birds* (New York: North Point Press, 2000).

## 21. Bloodroot

John Bartram's surviving letter to Ann is in *The Correspondence of John Bartram*.

## 23. The Lady Petre Pear Tree

Joel T. Fry gives details of the soil in Bartram's Garden in "Archaeological Research at Historic Bartram's Garden," *Bartram Broadside* (summer, 1998). Mark Laird describes Lord Petre and his garden in *The Flowering of the Landscape Garden: English Pleasure Grounds, 1720–1800* (Philadelphia: University of Pennsylvania Press, 1999). The postcards I discuss are from Dennis Lebofsky, unpublished postcard collection.

## 24. Zinnia

E. C. Pielou's meditations on water can be found in *Fresh Water* (Chicago: The University of Chicago Press, 1998).

## 25. Snowdrops

Bartram's detailed weather observations are in his annotated almanacs at the Academy of Natural Sciences, Philaldelphia.

## 28. Mint

Ann Leighton quotes Abigail Adams's letter in *American Gardens of the Eighteenth Century* (1986).

## 29. Sunflower

Details of John Bartram's journey are in John Bartram, Lewis Evans, and Conraid Weiser, *A Journey From Pennsylvania to Onondaga in 1743* (Barre, Mass.: Imprint Society, 1973); William H. Goetzmann, "John Bartram's Journey to Onondaga in Context" in *America's Curious Botanist, A Tercentennial Reappraisal of John Bartram 1699–1777* (Philadelphia: American Philosophical Society, 2004); James H. Merrell, *Into the American Woods* (New York: Norton, 1999); and Slaughter, *The Natures of John and William Bartram*. Mark Laird includes information on John Bartram's expeditions and garden in *The Flowering of the Landscape Garden*.

## 30. Poinsettia

All descriptions of nineteenth-century gardens are from James Boyd, *A History of the Pennsylvania Horticultural Society, 1827–1927* (Philadelphia: Pennsylvania Horticultural Society, 1929). Details of Bartram's Garden are in Joel T. Fry, "The Pond at Bartram's Garden," *Bartram Broadside* (summer 1997). Information about Ann Carr's life is included in Slaughter, *The Natures of John and William Bartram*, and Smith, "The Bartram Women."

## 32. Gingko

John Bartram's will can be found in the archives at Bartram's Garden, Philadelphia.

### GLADWYNE

## 33. Auricula

Deborah Logan's descriptions of her family's garden when she was a child are in *The Norris House* (N.p.: Fairhill-Press, 1867). Details of the rural life of Isaac Norris Sr. are in his annotated almanacs at The Library Company of Philadelphia. Quotations from the letters of Isaac Norris and his daughter Deborah, as well as details of his house and gardens, are from Mark Reinberger and Elizabeth McLean, "Isaac Norris's Fairhill: Architecture, Landscape, and Quaker Ideals in a Philadelphia Colonial Country Seat,"

*Winterthur Portfolio* 32 no. 4 (winter 1997). Letitia E. Wright discusses William Logan's garden in *Colonial Garden at Stenton Described in Old Letters* (Philadelphia: Pennsylvania Horticultural Society, 1916).

### 34. Violets

Saint Catherine's life is included in David Hugh Farmer, *The Oxford Dictionary of Saints* (New York: Oxford University Press, 1982). Details of medieval gardens and gardeners are in John Harvey, *Mediaeval Gardens* (Beaverton, Ore.: Timber Press, 1981).

### 36. Honeysuckle

Peter Bernhardt, *The Rose's Kiss: A Natural History of Flowers* (Chicago: University of Chicago Press, 2000). The quote on page 180 is from Maureen Carroll, *Earthly Paradises: Ancient Gardens in History and Archaeology* (Los Angeles: J. Paul Getty Museum, 2003).

### 37. Franklinia

Joel T. Fry, "*Franklinia alatamaha*, A History of That 'Very Curious' Shrub," *Bartram Broadside* (spring 2000). Mary Gibson Henry's life is described in Mary Harrison, "Mary Gibson Henry, Plantswoman Extraordinaire," *Arnoldia* 60 no. 1 (2000); Mary Gibson Henry, "An Autobiography," *Herbertia* 6 (1950); and Mary Gibson Henry, "Collecting Plants Beyond the Frontier in Northern British Columbia," *National Horticulture Magazine* (1934-35). William Robinson, *The Wild Garden* (Portland, Ore.: Sagapress/Timber Press, 1994).